The Dynamics of Motivating Prospects to Buy

The Dynamics of Motivating Prospects to Buy

H. B. Rames

Parker Publishing Company, Inc.
West Nyack, New York

Library of Congress Cataloging in Publication Data

Rames, H B
The dynamics of motivating prospects to buy.

1. Salesmen and salesmanship. I. Title.
HF5438.R26 658.85 73-7858
ISBN 0-13-222133-0

Printed in the United States of America

Foreword

Here is a thought-provoking and powerful treatment of both the art and tools of selling.

Hank Rames is that rare "man for all seasons," a salesman's salesman and an educator's educator. He is equally at home in a no-holds-barred sales meeting, a university lecture class or an eyeball–to–eyeball selling opportunity.

It is my privilege to recommend this thorough and useful book to all sales people who are committed to growth and success.

There's something here for all.

Joe Batten
President
Batten, Batten, Hudson & Swab, Inc.

What the Dynamic Sales Laws Will Do For You

The sales techniques in this book have been proven through extensive application and might be called "new"; yet they have existed since man first sold a new stone ax to his neighbor. You may have unconsciously used them from time to time and, therefore, you have the potential ability to put them into *conscious* use and realize their early rewards. They are now becoming formally recognized and, in this book, they are organized into a body of knowledge known as *The Dynamic Sales Laws.*

The Dynamic Sales Laws can help you to:

1. **Sell More Prospects.** You are probably a conscientious salesman—honest and energetic. This being so, your sales day might go something like this: Out of ten calls you make in a day, two prospects buy voluntarily; another two prospects buy as a result of your actions and words; and six don't buy. Possibly, your close ratio is different; but the fact remains that too many prospects get away.

   The Dynamic Sales Laws will help you salvage many of the prospects that "get away" by explaining how to analyze prospects and how to develop each sale. Properly used, these principles will help you select better prospects to serve as the nucleus of your sales program and will ensure sales techniques that result in more sales.

2. **Sell with More Satisfaction.** One of the most important of the recent findings in the behavioral sciences is the discovery that

those persons who receive the greatest satisfactions for their work are the most productive.

The philosophy underlying the Dynamic Sales Laws gives a new perspective to selling—one that is a stimulating substitute to the monotony of sales calls. As a consequence of putting this new sales system to work for you, new vitality will be yours.

This is probably what will happen: You will call on more tough prospects. You will increase your close ratio. You will increase your sales calls. Why? Because you will sell more? Only partially. It will happen chiefly because you are going to develop a sales procedure that works—that allows you to perform at your best.

3. **Sell with Confidence.** For years, sales managers have admonished their salesmen to "stay in control." They and most salesmen interpret this advice to mean "keep talking"—don't permit the prospect to assume too prominent a place in the conversation. The Dynamic Sales Laws contend that quite the opposite is preferable.

   The Dynamic Sales Laws use various methods to get the prospect to talk. The salesman stays in control because he asks the questions and ultimately leads the prospect to the close. Confidence is born of knowing your sales strategy—where you are going with each prospect. Confidence is born of knowing the techniques that lead to the sale.

4. **Sell with Professionalism.** Selling is more than talking, just as scoring a touchdown is more than running, blocking and throwing the ball. The difference between "going through the motions" and winning the game is having a strategy that works. Strategy in football is often knowing the opposing team's weaknesses and strengths and then encouraging the other team to execute its weaknesses, and supressing or avoiding the opportunities for it to show its strengths.

   A professional salesman follows a similar strategy or game plan. He knows the strength of the prospect is his ever-present capability to say "No." He learns that the prospect's "weaknesses" are his internal motivations; and these he gets out in the open. The Dynamic Sales Laws will make any salesman a "pro" by providing the framework for him to develop his game plan.

As you go forward in this book, remind yourself that selling is a *mental* activity; it is not an athletic event calling for the physical endurance to make ten to twenty sales calls a day. Nor is it a speaking contest to determine how many product features you can recite in ten minutes. It is a mental activity based on the Dynamic Sales Laws—laws that are immutable—proved by extensive research. They will work for you—in *your* way, with *your* prospects, for *your* products.

—*Hank Rames*

Table of Contents

The Dynamics of Motivating Prospects to Buy

1

How to Make the Changing, Dynamic Marketplace Work for You

There is probably nobody more flexible, more accustomed to change than the salesman. That's what we feed on. That's what adds zest to our days.

That's what this book is about—change. That's what makes it *dynamic*. Most of us think "dynamic" means "tremendous" or "great"—an adjective we apply to a product or idea that is a big breakthrough in technology. Not so. Dynamic means "effective action on bodies in motion or at rest." A force, to be dynamic, must set a body in motion from a stand-still, or accelerate a body already in motion. It's a moving force, an effective action. And that in itself implies change.

What's in It for You?

Maybe a nagging voice in the corner of your mind keeps saying, "There must be a better way to sell. I work hard and I work long. Admittedly I don't handle all situations well. But is the answer to be found only in working harder and longer?" If you're tormented with this doubt, hang in there; we're going to arrive at some startling conclusions.

It is absolutely not necessary to sell harder or longer to use the Dynamic Laws of Motivation. Actually, quite the reverse is true. If you are an experienced salesman, you will know that what I have to say is true. The beginning salesman must take my word for it. Many professional salesmen who possess this knowledge and have converted it to practice do not work as hard as the average salesman; yet they earn two, three or more times as much. They have a sixth sense that seems to lead them to where the business is. This extrasensory perception allows them to close a high percentage of their sales calls. They get referrals automatically, they sell easily, effortlessly—without pressure! They enjoy great rapport with their customers.

You can pull yourself from the humdrum, routine, lackluster *work* of selling to a new plateau of pleasure and reward with the Dynamic Laws of Motivation; and I promise you there will be no table pounding, no exhortations to "Sell Enthusiastically," no canned sales presentations. You will not be asked to make a complete turnabout in your present procedures.

The only thing I ask is that you THINK. After all, selling is essentially a *mental* activity. This book has not been written for all salesmen: I'm talking only to the salesmen who are willing to really *think*. This is the only concession I ask you to make.

Start Living As a Change Agent

Ever think of yourself as a "change agent"? That's what you are, really. On every sales call, you urge people to change: "Buy from me instead of my competitor,"—"Buy in larger quantities" (instead of small token orders)—"Buy this new product"—(instead of conventional items). You don't say these words, but they represent your intent, don't they? You want to bring about change.

In communication with your employer, again you act as a change agent: "I could write more business if our price were more competitive"—"My territory is too large" (or too small)—"We need more advertising on the ABC line." Again you want to bring about change.

Salesmen are probably more intimately concerned with bringing about change than members of any other occupational group. It is strange, therefore, that so many salesmen resist making changes in themselves. Often, poor sales volume is attributed to the prospect (he couldn't see a good deal if he met one), the product (overpriced), the advertising support (nobody's ever heard of the company) or the territory (low-income people won't buy). However, these usually are not the areas in which change is most urgently needed.

What kind of changes are we talking about? What we must change is behavior: what one does (or doesn't do), what one says (or doesn't say). This is an important point, as we shall see when we discuss the scientific basis of these Dynamic Laws. The beginning of wisdom is analysis; so let's start by analyzing why people resist change.

Why Don't People Change More Easily?

Why do your customers (and you and me) grow inflexible, fall into ruts? Often we're unhappy with the way things are. Suddenly a new experience (a new product, a new way to sell, a new business opportunity) breaks into our lives and we hang back. Why?

"I don't know. Guess I just didn't think," replied Stanley Sands. I had been working with Stan on a new closing technique for selling insurance, but on the first call we made after our discussion, he fell back into his old habit of saying "Well, if you need more information, just call." *Not thinking* cost Stan over $50 in time lost, and a lot more if we consider his share of the premium had he closed the call.

The failure to think is a type of *inertia,* consigning us to inactivity and mediocrity unless it is overcome. William James, the American psychologist, said that most of us, by the time we are 25, are virtually "a bundle of habits." Stan had trod the ground of "if you need more information, just call" so often, he was in a rut. Under the stress of a sales situation, this familiar phrase just rolled out, "without thinking."

"I've always wanted to advance in this company," an older production worker told me. "Dad was sales manager, you know. I worked with him in sales for several summers while I was going to school and I don't know when I've enjoyed anything so much. Now? Well, there's lots of problems in sales. I know I can run this turret lathe and I don't worry about it." This, Gilbert Murray calls "failure of nerve."

Many mature men try to rationalize their resistance to change and, in so doing, blind themselves to the vulnerability of their position. Lynn White Jr. said it:

> We live in an era when rapid change breeds fear and fear too often congeals us into rigidity, which we mistake for stability.

We'll talk more about change throughout this book, because the central theme of the Dynamic Laws is focused on bringing about behavior changes in your customers through your observance of certain psychological laws. I have introduced the problem of change into our early discussion because I want you to anticipate it as a problem when the laws are introduced to you. Although I expect you will resist changing your sales behavior, I want to be completely honest with you and urge you to recognize this resistance for what it is when you encounter it. We are creatures of habit and we fear the risk of new methods; but if we expect our customers to change, is it, after all, too much to ask that *we* be willing to change too?

You Hold the Key to Selling More Effectively

Much of what I'm going to say to you about selling more effectively you probably already know; but I'm going to cause you to examine your knowledge of human nature in a different way, to discover the truths that lie hidden, to bring elements of your experience out into the open so that we can extract from them a procedure that makes sense to you—and to the prospect.

A simple analogy may help in this analysis. Consider the principles that control the flow of water through a water system. The output of water can be increased in two ways: We can increase the pressure by erecting a standpipe or phasing a pump into the system; or we can increase the size of the pipes. Both you and your prospect have felt the pressures of "power closes," of forceful persuasion, of competing products—pressures that build to a danger point. The alternative is clear: you must look to your personal development—enlarging the pipes—as the only logical means toward multiplying your output.

Personal development is well within your capacity. Based on behavioral principles that have been more intensively researched than perhaps any other business science in modern times, the development of a body of sales knowledge can result in new confidence and professional recognition for you.

How Behavioral Science Can Lead You to a New Understanding of People

Behavioral Science is a relatively new science; however, almost 50 years of research and practical application have given us a large body of knowledge that concerns itself with how and why people behave in the ways they do. Such men as Eldon Mayo at Western Electric, B. F. Skinner at Harvard and, more recently, Douglas McGregor at M.I.T. have toppled some of the old "Drugstore Indians" that for years have hampered our progress in understanding human behavior.

Applied to selling, behavioral science holds that a salesman might know his *product* in depth, but unless he knows his *prospect* in depth, nothing much will happen. The prospect makes the buying decision based primarily on his *feelings,* not exclusively on the rational determinants of price, delivery, terms, etc. The salesman must develop techniques for getting a "feel for his prospect's feelings." Although you are probably one of the first to use these improved methods in your company and territory, you will join a rapidly-growing cadre of salesmen who are embracing this more productive way to sell. You will become a "pro" in every sense of the word.

When you possess a working knowledge of behavioral science principles, you will suddenly find it easier to sell—even to "difficult" prospects. You will be the "pro" I talked about at the beginning of this chapter: one who sells easily, effortlessly, with no pressure.

What the Pro Believes

Price Alone Is Never the Decisive Selling Point

This is probably the toughest concept for salesmen to accept. Why? Price is the fortress behind which prospects hide and defend themselves against frontal sales attacks and, because some companies can always make a product or provide a service of less quality and sell it cheaper, the prospect is in a strong defensive position.

If you sell on bid, as in construction materials, school supplies and heavy equipment, it is easy to justify less-than-adequate salesmanship by maintaining that "the lowest price gets the business." In most instances it does—until a "thinking" salesman comes along with a workable knowledge of why prospects buy and secures the larger part of the contract *at a higher price!*

Price serves another purpose. I recently conducted a sales seminar for a strongly research-oriented company in the drug field. Considerable time was spent in a "bull session" discussing a product the company had researched and marketed. Within three years of its market introduction, cheaper synthetic substitutes flooded the market. The company began losing its share of market. The question, according to the sales manager, was "How can we slow the loss trend on this product and increase sales?" The salesmen were eager to suggest ideas because they were paid a 5% commission on sales in addition to a salary. Salesman after salesman maintained that he couldn't increase sales, despite the product's superiority, because of "price." It wasn't until the sales manager demonstrated that by decreasing the price 25% (and in so doing, scrapping several features which gave the product its superiority), each salesman would have to sell 33⅓% more *just to break even,* that price became a less important sales determinant to the salesmen.

Do I maintain that price is *not* important? No, indeed. Price—*low* price—is important under these conditions:

1. Specials, close-outs, introductory offers, etc.: When a lower-than-normal price is offered, usually for a limited time on a standard product, the salesman, without delving any deeper into the buyer's motives, can trade on a lower price.

2. Sub-standard products: When a product is actually inferior to competitive products on the market, a lower price is usually the only inducement important enough to sell it.

3. Sub-standard salesmanship: When a salesman has not trained himself to search for the real reasons people buy, he doesn't see himself as a professional—as a motivator of buying action. Low price is the only way he can sell.

It will become apparent as we move forward into our discussion of the Dynamic Laws in relation to prospect motivation that price has primacy only to the salesman who is either not as good as he knows he can be or who is selling an inferior product.

The Reasons for Buying Are Found Not in What You Say, But in What the Prospect Says

I remember my astonishment as a boy when I made the acquaintance of a man who, in his first year as a car-accessory salesman, sold double the volume of any man on the sales force. The astonishing fact was that Clem had "country hick" written all over him—in his dress, his speech, his mannerisms. Clem once admitted he knew nothing about salesmanship. "And knowin' nothin'," he shrugged, "I jes' listen to the prospect." It wasn't until I met and worked with the famous Elmer ("Say It With Flowers") Wheeler, that anyone reduced this principle to a well-chosen word. Elmer used to point out that the best salesmen spend their time asking questions. Instead of making long speeches extolling the virtues of their product, they would let the prospect work on his favorite subject: himself. Then they would relate their product to what he had to say about himself.

In our heart of hearts, you and I regard ourselves as exceptional persons. We each have a unique set of likes and dislikes—the result of a lifetime of experience and living. This is true of prospects, too. With the billions of people on this earth, there are no two identically alike. The red convertible that "turns on" one teenager has no appeal to another. The exclusiveness of a home in the country–club section of the city appeals to one family but may be repulsive to another family. An advertising program that is "just what we're looking for" to one advertising manager is "way off base" to another. And so it goes.

This is why a canned sales talk which presumes that all prospects are alike doesn't get the job done. Sometimes a "standard pitch" is used in mass merchandising programs to sell Mr. Average Prospect. Nevertheless, the door-to-door or telephone sales contacts are always preceded by a thorough market research study. The creative salesman simply can't make presumptions about why an individual prospect will buy. He can, and should, make some assumptions prior to the call, but he should "test" them with each prospect. He does this by leading the prospect into a discussion of himself, his problems, the way he views a particular situation.

A canned presentation is seldom effective in creative salesmanship. This doesn't mean that the salesman can neglect to prepare for the sales call. It does mean that sales action must be directed toward geting the prospect to reveal his Achilles Heel—his reason for buying. The Dynamic Laws, when observed by the thinking, creative salesman, will allow him to practically "read the prospect's mind." The prospect will unconsciously reveal through his responses to questions how he can be sold or what hurdles must be overcome before the sale is made. The key is getting the prospect to talk.

The Prospect Buys Most Often Because of His Feelings Rather Than Logic

"More goods are bought from the heart than from the head." Hard to believe? Yes, indeed. In the social environment in which most of us live, from early childhood on, we have been told, "Boys don't cry" and "Don't blow your cool." Parents and teachers have forever been inventing ruses to spare the child from confrontations that may result in a show of "feelings." As adults, how few of us ever turn to our life's companion and say "I love you"! Emotions or feelings traditionally have been subjugated to reason and logic for fear that one's actions may be considered immodest, immature or imprudent. So it is small wonder that we grow up to distrust emotions and to place no great value in them as an important source of buying motivation. In addition to the need for feelings of confidence, esteem and recognition, there are the more common emotions of love, fear and laughter—all of which, in the words of Ardis Whitman, "hold enormous reservoirs of power . . . (but) day after day we leave this rich store of vitality untapped."

Think for a moment of the great power of emotion in determining buying behavior, in persuading people to a particular action. Charity drives depend on it. Political campaigns, much of the billion-dollar health industry and some aspects of the welfare program derive their immense power from "feelings." For example, several years ago, San Francisco's cable cars were held in contempt by

City Hall accountants as dangerous, out-worn liabilities. They were scheduled for the junk yard and new shiny buses were to be substituted. San Franciscans rose as one in protest. Reason and logic decreed that the streetcars should go: they cost too much and they were inefficient. But they were kept because of the love and affection of thousands. Today, you can still ride on the old, inadequate, obsolete money-losing pieces of last-century machinery because of the power of emotion.

An individual prospect may not be too "intelligent," but his heart is usually full of wants, needs and desires, and it's almost virgin territory for the enterprising salesman. Later in this book you will learn how to explore for these hidden emotional wants—security, esteem, belongingness, recognition, prestige, self-realization and others.

You can sell more to the heart than to the head.

The Ideal Prospect Is Seldom the Best Prospect

Sometimes, as we reflect on a particularly tough sales day, we imagine in our mind's eye a more ideal situation, a territory populated by ideal prospects: men who see us promptly when we call, who laugh at our jokes, who listen intently and never interrupt and, finally, who buy without a struggle! Ah, Utopia!

Most salesmen have a mental image of the ideal prospect. His characteristics may vary from salesman to salesman, but generally, he is a man we enjoy calling on, who doesn't give us too much "static," who helps fill out the call report. Unconsciously, we try to accumulate more of these types in our prospect stables and usually give them more attention and service than the other kind. The ancient Greeks, as usual, had some words for it. They said that human beings are constantly striving toward pleasure and avoidance of pain.

The question this raises is: Does the near-ideal prospect buy enough to warrant his dominant position, both as the objective of major sales emphasis and the recipient of extra attention? The answer is No.

Being easy to call on (and even enjoyable) makes him a popular target for your competitor as well. The fact that he usually has time to see you suggests that he isn't too busy, that his business might not be too good and, therefore, that he probably won't buy new items nor will he buy old items at a high volume level.

In your own stable of prospects, you can naturally point to exceptions to these two conditions. Nevertheless, the principle holds true: If you are the usual salesman, you are avoiding, overlooking, unconsciously neglecting important customers because they are difficult. You fill your day with as many friendly customers as possible and, in so doing, you are necessarily limiting your income and your opportunities to get ahead.

Let us analyze this dilemma. We have said that we probably neglect the difficult prospect. The question may seem to be: Why is he difficult? This problem statement we will reject. To explain his personality would require a lengthy psychological study. Since we can't significantly change his personality anyway, it would be a poor time investment. A better question is: Why do we neglect the difficult prospect?

We avoid difficult situations in life because we don't understand them. Think back on the courses with which you had difficulty in high school or college—Differential Equations for example. Chances are you thought of it as a difficult course until (hopefully) half way through, when it finally dawned on you what it was all about. Then it became enjoyable and challenging.

The difficult prospect has needs, desires and wants just as does the more ideal prospect. He is actually easier to sell to because fewer salesmen call on him and because his feelings are out in the open for you to observe and understand. Strive to understand his needs and sell to him the way he wants to be sold. The ability to understand is so rare that chances are he'll show his appreciation by giving you a giant share of his business.

How Your Prospect Regards Your Product May Bear Little Resemblance to What the Product Really Is

It is important to understand what a product means to a prospect before we try to sell it.

Usually our introduction to a new product consists of an extended product-orientation meeting or bulletin: a mass of details of how the product is researched, manufactured and marketed, with strong emphasis on how it works and how it is to be sold. These are the *mechanics* of the product.

To the consumer, the product usually means something quite different. It may mean a new life style, a new status, renewed confidence, greater acceptance, etc. People often buy because their lives have not given them gratification in certain social, intellectual or physical relations. They will be inclined to buy your product if they see in it a promise that certain of these wants may be satisfied. This is the *psychology* of the product.

It will be easy for you to dispute these statements. Much of your sales life has dealt with the "mechanics," and almost all of the company's sales training is concerned with "mechanics." The prospect asks product-information questions. He advances product features to justify his reasons for buying or not buying. In sales conversations, the psychological aspects of the product are rarely mentioned. Therefore, your question, "Does this law of buying motivation always apply?" is a good one. The answer is Yes; however, it varies in importance in relation to the characteristics of the product, the market, the prospect and the salesman. But it is always present.

For example, a superficial examination of industrial selling would lead us to believe that a firm buys a product that fills "the specs," when all details of availability, delivery, credit terms, etc., are satisfied. These rational requirements are indeed necessary, but competition in most industries is so keen today that *most companies meet these rational requirements*. Therefore, they lose their importance, and the decision to buy is often made on the basis of the image the buyers have of you, your product and your company.

The salesmen who look for and find the image of how each prospect interprets their product in terms of satisfaction of his psychological wants and then subtly appeals to that want have a critical advantage over the prospect.

Dr. Ernest Dichter,* President of the Institute for Motivational Research, Croton-on-Hudson, New York, and one of the foremost authorities on buying motivation, puts it well when he says:

---

* Ernest Dichter, Ph.D., *Handbook of Consumer Motivations* (New York, N.Y. McGraw-Hill Book Co., 1964) p. 4.

> A bedraggled column of refugees struggle down the muddy road, their backs bent under their few meager possessions. A few pieces of clothing, sometimes a mattress, or even a sewing machine stick out weirdly. They mean life to people. Some of the things are important for survival; most of them, however, such as a child's doll or the long faded and useless wedding dress of the woman are a tangible anchorage, an accent on life's continuity. They are needed for the glow they give, however weak, in the bottomless darkness of human despair. Hollow hands clasp ludicrous posessions because they are the links in the chain of life. If it breaks, they are truly lost.

The Principal Reason People Don't Buy Is That They Don't Listen

There's a difference between "hearing" and "listening." Hearing is paying attention with the *ear;* listening is paying attention with the *mind.*

Most prospects are poor listeners. Furthermore, they do not listen effectively to sales presentations. It's a wonder we sell as much as we do! Why do prospects fail to really listen? Well, several reasons:

First, the salesman is an interrupter of his routine. The prospect may continue to think about the problem that was occupying his attention prior to the sales call and not give his full mental resources to what the salesman says. (More on this in Chapter 9.) Also, he is probably not as adept in the skill of listening as he is in reading or speaking. These reasons may serve to explain his deficiency; however, since we can do little to change his listening habits in one sales call, we'll have to look elsewhere.

Several weeks ago, I attended a committee meeting during which a government official reviewed the progress of his department in meeting the park and recreational needs of the people of his state. Although the report was very complete, I found myself thinking of other things as the charts of statistical comparisons continued to unfold. He failed completely in his communication to me because he talked solely from his point of view and interpreted none of his material into areas of interest to the members of the state and community. I am sure he had valuable things to say, but they escaped me because I wasn't listening.

Ralph Nichols, Professor at the University of Minnesota, has perhaps done more than any other individual in America to make us conscious of the rewards of improving our listening skills. Dr. Nichols tells of his experience as a young boy in attending church. He would prepare for each Sunday by setting aside various things to think about as the pastor talked. Therefore, the time would not be entirely wasted.

Conversely, which speeches and presentations do you recall to which you really listened and, thus, can remember even to this day? Probably the utterances of Churchill—"I have nothing to offer but blood, toil, tears and sweat"—or Roosevelt—"Let me assert my firm belief that the only thing we have to fear is fear itself." These men and others literally forced people to listen because they made contact with their inner needs and wants.

If our prospects were better listeners, they would probably buy more from us. But because most of them are not skilled and trained in the art of listening, it is incumbent on you to cause them to listen by allowing them to see the satisfaction of their inner needs and wants or the solution to a problem through your product.

Prospects don't listen to a recitation of the features of a product; however, they have no other alternative but to listen when they can sense how your product will permit them to enjoy a better life.

The Reasons for Buying or Not Buying Advanced by Most Prospects Are Not Their Real Reasons

We all experience a comedy of buying motivation similar to the man who didn't "have the money" to buy a new set of needed tires for his car but who did have $2,000 to trade in his old car on a new Super Sport. The reason he advanced for not buying the unglamorous tires was, "I don't have the money"—a reason that obviously doesn't hold water when he pictures himself behind the wheel of his new Super Sport. Ask him why he bought the Super Sport and his reply will probably be "The old jalopy was wearing out"—again not his real reason.

According to authorities, women buy that intimate item of apparel called a bra so that they may be more attractive sexually. Confront a woman with that reason and you're in deep trouble!

You have wondered why women buy mini-skirts one season, the next season go to long dresses and, who knows, the next season the mini- or midi-skirt is back. Big hats, small hats or no hats follow in rapid succession. You may argue: "The short dress or the large hat is more attractive, and it isn't worn out, so why buy another style?" But men are no different. Chances are, you will wear slim pants, flare pants or hip pants, single-breasted coats or double-breasted, wide lapels or slim lapels, wide or narrow ties, etc. etc. There is a very definite social reason for this madness, which none of us will admit to ourselves, namely: The up-to-date dressers belong, or want to belong, to a particular social class. The others, who wear outdated, old-fashioned apparel, belong to another. The image of the fashionable is that of progressive, active, modern leaders; the image of the others is that of staid, conservative, plodding followers. But do we admit to these reasons? Absolutely not.

Over a period of several months, my next-door neighbor spent over $700 in buying an assortment of power tools for his workshop. The rational reason he gave to his wife for his large financial outlay was that the power tools would allow him to save money. "Now," he said, "I do most of the repairs around the house and make things I can't afford to buy." Being a smart politician, his first project was a sewing center for his wife. After buying all the wood, hardware and a few drills, his saving was $17! But he earned the accolades of his wife and friends that "Harry is very handy around the house." I can still see him with that expression of utter omnipotence as he "rips" a piece of lumber with his new circular saw!

Why is this? Why do we shield our real reasons for buying or not buying? Why does the prestige-seeking family that buys into a plush neighborhood say, "It was such a good bargain; we couldn't turn it down?" Why do we decline to buy and advance a false reason?

In the culture in which most of us have been reared, the inner drives have somehow been labeled as unhealthy or even sinful. For example, pride has been considered the "sin of the Angels." Mothers once tsk tsk'd "Envy not, want not," but envy has persisted so strongly that today we sweeten this inner drive by calling it "keeping up with the Joneses." Sloth has all but lost its original sinful connotation in the mass rush to introduce time-saving devices that herald in the sought-for era of leisure time. Even anger (although not usually a buying motive) has reached a plateau of respectability as psychiatry intones patients to "let it out."

But we remain in the shadow of our culture. People don't level with each other partly because of the tainted morality of inner drives and the fear of embarrassment. Also, we don't want to give the other guy an advantage.

You, as a salesman, can become aware of the enormous power exerted by these inner drives. No prospect is going to tell you he wants prestige or security or recognition; but there are certain clues that will lead you to identification of these wants as powerful selling appeals. Knowledge of these drives will assist you as does a map in arriving at your destination, without being thrown off target by false reasons.

FOR THE NEXT WEEK . . .

Be alert to these new concepts introduced in this chapter. Observe, analyze and think.

1. People tell us they want change because it's synonymous with progress, and yet they resist it. Compile a mental list of the reasons they give for not changing. How many of these reasons are valid? What are the *real* reasons?
2. Of the three "faces" of selling—product, prospect and salesman—which face do you least understand? Which one holds the key to better selling?
3. Price alone is never the decisive selling point. How many times during the week has "Your price is too high" been mentioned? Each time try to analyze. What is the real reason?
4. The reasons for buying are found not in what you say, but in what the prospect says. Keep a mental note of the proportion of the total interview time during which you talk against the time during which the prospect talks. Are you giving him sufficient opportunity to "open up"—to tell you how he can be sold?
5. The prospect buys most often because of his feelings rather than logic. Observe how often our logical reasons for buying seem-

ingly fall on deaf ears. When there seems to be a dominant logical reason, look for an inner need that motivates buying action.

6. The ideal prospect is seldom the best prospect. How many times during the week did you almost unconsciously overlook the difficult prospect? Out of your total calls, how many prospects are simply "nice guys"?
7. How your prospect regards your product may bear little resemblance to what the product really is. Look for the hidden reasons people buy (or do not buy).
8. The principal reason people don't buy is that they don't listen. Test frequently to determine if your prospect is listening. Do it with a question that can't be answered "Yes" or "No."
9. The reasons for buying or not buying advanced by most prospects are not their real reasons. Most salesmen don't know for sure why prospects buy. Try to discover why. The reasons they give are usually superficial ones. What are the real reasons?

2

How the Dynamic Sales Laws Came to Be As Effective As They Are Now

What exists today is by necessity the product of yesterday. The sales style that you use is the result of both adoptions of ideas you have gleaned from sales books, sales meetings and sales supervisors and adaptions or modifications you have learned from the crucible of experience. All actions and decisions regarding your sales procedures have been taken in the past and by necessity are based on the knowledge and materials available at that time. The people who have helped you mold your sales style—fellow salesmen, sales managers and customers—grew up in the business of yesterday.

As a consequence, we all tend to apply the lessons of the past to today. No matter how wise, forward-looking or courageous the sales style that you now employ was when it was first formulated, it has been overtaken by new events, by a new breed of buyers, by new methods of buying and selling.

This, of course, is true with many procedures in business. The world that made them no longer exists.

You probably recognize another problem: the reluctance of people to change. As opinions are based on past experiences, change is hard to bring about. *Time* * magazine gives us a good illustration:

---

* Reprinted by permission from *Time, The Weekly Newsmagazine;* © Time Inc., 1971.

> It is unlikely that any major enterprise was ever undertaken without an expert arguing conclusively that it would not succeed. At the behest of King Ferdinand and Queen Isabella, a panel of Spanish sages looked at Columbus' plan for a voyage to the Indies, and in 1490 came up with six good reasons why it was impossible. So many centuries after the creation, they concluded triumphantly, it was unlikely that anyone could find hitherto unknown lands.

In this chapter, I want to trace for you the evolution of a sales presentation so that you can understand why today's sales procedures came into being. With this understanding, I believe you will be less reluctant to make minor adjustments in your present procedures. My enthusiasm for the Dynamic Laws of Motivating Prospects is borne out of a sincere conviction that if you practice and use them, a whole new world of effective selling will open up to you.

How Do You Rate?

Before we review the evolution of a sales presentation, you may enjoy taking a short sales quiz. This quiz may serve to point out where you stand on sales presentations.

Here are two scrambled sales presentations. They proceed from 1 to 2 to 3, etc. Select the paragraph following the letter (a or b) that you feel is more salesworthy.

1. (a) Mr. Brown, I have an idea for you.

   (b) Hello, Mr. Brown. It's a lovely day isn't it? If you have a few minutes, I'd like to show you something our company has just come out with . . .

2. (a) The Widget is a clever gadget which has a sliding gear in the retrograde position . . .

   (b) Snarled assembly lines and irritations are smoothed out and production rates materially increased with Widget. Let me show you how.

3. (a) How do you feel about this feature? Will it prove useful to you?

   (b) Pardon me for interrupting, but here is something I don't want to forget . . .

4. (a) Will it work? You don't think my company would make 10,000 of 'em unless they did?
   (b) The efficiency of Widget is illustrated by the experience of the Condon Company, which last month . . .

5. (a) I can readily appreciate your reason for being hesitant. As I understand it, you feel that . . .
   (b) No. So and So's product doesn't begin to compare. Why they don't even plate the shim . . .

6. (a) Are you sure you haven't any more questions? Will you call me if you want more information?
   (b) Which model will better serve your needs: the unfinished or the chrome-plated?

Here are the better answers: 1a, 2b, 3a, 4b, 5a, 6b.
What Your Score Means:

Correct	Grade
6	Excellent
5	Good
4	Fair
3	Poor

The Conventional Sales Presentation Saddles a Salesman with Mediocrity

SALESMAN: Good afternoon, Mr. Brown. Bill Jones with Acme.
PROSPECT: How do you do? Sit down. What can I do for you?
SALESMAN: As your company is one of the leading concerns in this area, I thought you might be interested in our Subliminated Phasic Optimum Operant Frigerant (small laugh) S-P-O-O-F, or as we call it, Spoof. Get it? (another laugh)
PROSPECT: Yes, I get it. Why should I be interested?
SALESMAN: Because it is one of the few substances that can exist simultaneously in all three phases: liquid, gas and solid. A unique compound that is colorless and odorless with a density 1½ times that of air.
PROSPECT: You want me to buy something I can't see?
SALESMAN: Why not? You can't see your overhead, but it's there. And SPOOF is 15 times more efficient than its closest competitor. You see, due to an unusual

manufacturing process, Acme can produce SPOOF triple compressed and cooled.

The liquid is compressed to over 70 times normal pressure and temperature lowered to well under 60 degrees *below* zero centigrade. It is then sprayed into the expansion chamber. You know, of course, as pressure is released, a substance will cool. In this case the solid state emerges. The end product is compressed into blocks—just the right size for you to handle.

PROSPECT: Yes, but, how do I know . . .

SALESMAN: . . . whether the product is pure? That we check the quality? Have no fear, Acme is a leader in the field with many years experience, 12 plants to serve you and a college-trained quality control engineer at each. We stand behind SPOOF. Do you have any more questions?

PROSPECT: What does this miraculous substance cost?

SALESMAN: What does it cost? I thought you'd never ask (laugh). I'll give you a deal. I'll let you have it for two cents a pound.

PROSPECT: That's pretty expensive isn't it?

SALESMAN: No, actually it's quite low because of our recycling. Only 30% of the liquid enters the solid state in the expansion chamber. We recycle about 60% of the liquid through recompression to save you money. So we pass on an efficiency ratio of 3 to 60. Normally the price is closer to 5¢ a pound.

PROSPECT: But I can't use something I can't see—even at 2¢ a pound.

SALESMAN: Glad you brought that up. In cooperation with the nation's ecology efforts and to help clean up the environment, we give you another benefit. Any SPOOF you have left—any you don't use or sell—simply disapears! Now about price, if we cut it would you be interested?

PROSPECT: Sorry. You've been very entertaining. But frankly, I'm just not interested.

Of course, I'm poking a little fun at the conventional sales presentation. *Spoof* (Subliminated Plastic Optimum Operant Frigerant) is dry ice, carbon dioxide in the solid state—15 times colder than "our closest competitor"—ice. But it isn't too far fetched.

Take, for example, this excerpt from a recorded life insurance presentation:

> Now, let's see, you have four children, haven't you? You can include one or all four in your basic policy and extend the same percentage discount to their policies. If full premiums are paid during twenty years, the policy can be surrendered for a paid-up policy at face value. Of course this assumes that all coupons are surrendered at that time. In other words, they earn an advanced premium deposit of 3%, and funds can be withdrawn at any time.

This is an example of a product-rich agent delivering a prospect-poor presentation.

Several years ago, my wife decided she needed a small, lightweight vacuum cleaner to carry up the stairs to the bedrooms. Together, we visited a good department store in town and explained her need to the salesman. We even went into detail to explain a medical problem she had—"low back pain." As nearly as I can reconstruct his sales story, here it is:

> This is our finest canister cleaner. It features two speeds: the low speed for curtains and upholstery and the high speed for your rugs. There's a 2⅞ horse power motor to provide suction and to operate the vibrator—to beat the dirt out. The tools are carried on the top and the off/on switch is here. These bumpers won't allow the canister to scar your furniture and the case is all steel construction. It's heavy and rugged for long life.

This retail salesman is saying: "I don't care what *your* requirements are, I've spent too much time learning my sales story to change."

At one time, I was in the cattle-feeding business. I wanted to fatten some steers to get them ready to sell at the peak of the market, which was calculated to be in six weeks. A good commercial feed generally fattens more rapidly than the pasture grass I had been feeding them. So I called a reputable company in the feed business and a salesman was promptly sent out to see me. I told him specifically what I wanted—not just once, but three times during the sales presentation! He was not to be deterred from what *he thought* I should hear: He showed me a map pinpointing their twelve plants and twenty-seven offices "within easy reach to serve you better." Another brochure was used to show me their new grinding and processing equipment. I interrupted from time to time (rather weakly toward the end, I fear) to present my problem. Once I even said, "I don't care about all your plants. What will the feed do for my cattle?" As close as he ever came to solving my problem was when he said, "It should do pretty well. I sell a lot of it." He said to me in effect: "I won't let you buy my feed until you accept the fact that my company is best because we have 12 plants and 27 offices."

This reminds me of another story. I do not know its source, but it is, nevertheless, a classic.

A salesman addressed himself to a farmer:

> Yes sir, this is the very latest down on the farm. The sisal fiber of these straw hats is grown on the mountain slopes of Ecuador—not just *any* mountain slope, mind you, only those facing the east to catch the morning sun. As a result, the fiber is more supple and doesn't crack when it is woven by the Ecuadorian weavers, who are hand picked and must have over five years' experience before they are allowed to work on such a high-quality hat as this. The crown is exactly 2¾ inches high so that an air dead space is formed between your head and the crown. The brim is 3¼ inches wide, so that you can start plowing as early as 6:15 in the morning and work as late as 7 in the evening without adjusting your hat to avoid sunglare or neck burn. See this decorative ribbon? It's made of genuine Parisian lamé imported especially for us. The sweat-band is . . .

The farmer interrupted to ask:

> Tell me, young fellow, will the darn thing keep the sun out of my eyes?

This salesman is really saying: "I love the sound of my voice, don't you?"

Don't Kid Yourself

I believe the hardest thing that anybody has to do in life is to be completely honest with one's self. I don't know you. I wish I did. In the absence of any real knowledge of you, I must merely state some facts and hope that you have the strength to look at yourself with as much detachment as you can, to objectively appraise the kind of sales procedures you use. If you will do that, the battle is half won and I'll pick it up from there.

Much sales performance is largely wasteful because it is not purposeful. The sales presentations I have just given you are wasteful because they obscured the real purpose of a salesman. His purpose is not to do all the talking or even a major part of it. Despite the fact that the real purpose of a sales call can be stressed by the prospect several times, some salesman will ignore it and pursue a counterfeit purpose of their own, choosing to "load" the sales presentation with product features, technical information or company propaganda.

Any salesman eager to improve his sales deportment must analyze his present procedures and, if he *in all honesty* finds them lacking, he must make some key decisions. Did you, for example, find a little bit of yourself in the sales presentations just given to you? When key decisions are made regarding your true objectives, the excellence you require, the priorities on which you will concentrate—then you begin to *sell for results.*

It is natural that there should be some disagreement as to what is good and bad sales technique. So that you can learn why certain techniques are used and why there exists natural disagreement on what are good or bad techniques, we are going to review the development of the technique of selling. As we do so, I will introduce you to a new, more effective and easier way to sell.

Galileo proposed that the sun was the center of the universe. This didn't change anything; but it gave us greater insight into many natural phenomena. Later in this chapter, I'm going to propose to you a new concept of selling that will give you greater insight and will serve to make your work more effective.

How the Puritan Ethics School Contributes to Your Success and Yet Is Ineffective

Salesman have always been told that they should reflect the qualities of enthusiasm, honesty and hard work. Most of us were brought

DIAGRAM 2.1

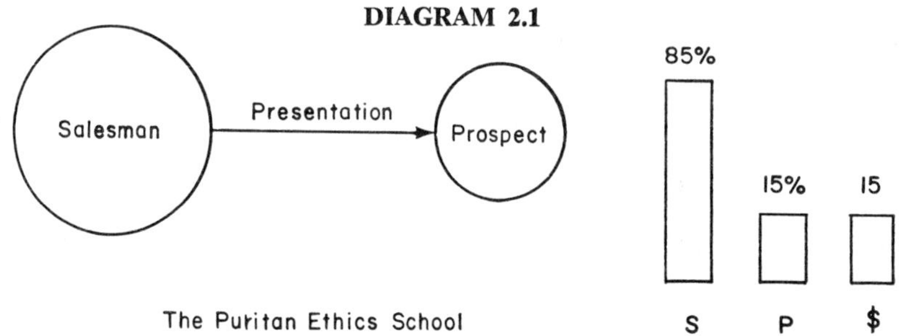

The Puritan Ethics School

up this way, for we live in a largely moral environment. These qualities and others comprise the Puritan Ethics, which at one time were thought to be the only necessary prerequisites for success. Fifty to 75 years ago, most people (salesmen included) were apathetic toward work. The big successes in the business world at the turn of the century took the Puritan Ethics to heart and, with a bit of imagination and inventive genius, soared to the top. (It might be interesting to debate how they might fare in today's world.) The Puritan Ethics served to make business people hardworking.

It was during this period that sales managers drilled home the admonitions: *Stay in control . . . Be dynamic . . . Talk faster than the prospect . . . Be forceful . . . If a need doesn't exist, convince 'em of one . . . Close 'em hard . . . Don't take any back-talk*. Talk became the salesman's stock in trade. He attracted attention with his sailor straw hat, his button shoes, his flamboyant suit, his suitcase full of dirty laundry and his mind full of dirty stories.

We poke fun at this salesman today: the back slapper, the fast talker, the guy who "could sell a farmer a milking machine and take his two cows as a down payment." Fortunately, "the peddler" has long ago left the sales scene, but some of his habits—for better and for worse—linger on. For instance, hard work: *Nothing wrong with hard work if it is purposeful.* But making the call quota of ten calls just on the outside chance that you can find a "hot" one or that the law of averages will work for you is absurd. Now, I believe in hard work as much as the next guy; but I insist that I work hard only when I can make my work count for something.

You have to stay in control is another carryover. In those days (and unfortunately today for many salesmen) this meant that you had to do all the talking. "Don't let the customer talk, for he may ask you a question."

Talk fast, be forceful might be translated to mean "make such a pest of yourself that he'll buy just to get rid of you."

Close 'em hard selling was a contest to see who was mightier. After all, the salesman wouldn't be back for six months, so why not?

I told you we must Sell for Results, so how did this "out-of-town jasper" do? Diagram 2.1 points out the characteristics of the Puritan School. The spotlight is on the salesman as the most important member of the triad. The prospect, you will observe, plays a minor role, as does the presentation. The salesman talks 85% of the time; the prospect is limited to only 15% participation. You will find, however, that the prospect gets even, as in this example, in which only 15 out of 100 contracts were sold.

Why a "Product Pitch" Brings You Only Half-Way Home

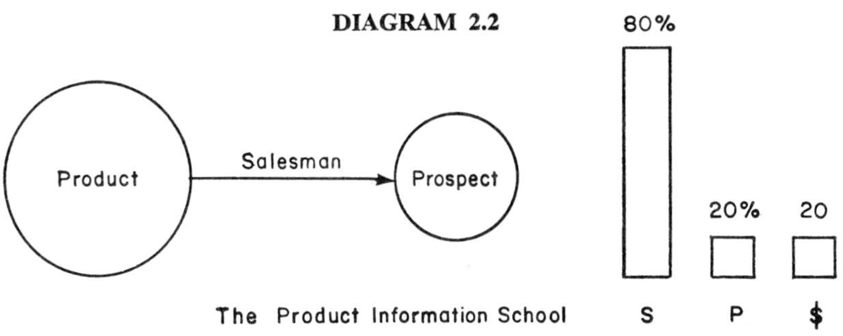

As our industries began to enlarge and handled more products and the number of competing companies increased, we began to hear a lot about "product differentials." We had to sell the features of our product that made it better than our competitor's; so most training time was spent in product information. Top management became complacent. All they needed was the best product on the market and sales would take care of themselves. It was this trend that built the enormous research staffs of modern companies.

In the sales field, the result was the development of men who were walking encyclopedias of information and statistics. Their sales presentations were uninterrupted, in-depth reviews of their products. At the conclusion, the prospect either bought (if he was still awake) or he didn't buy (because he simply stopped listening).

This "Product–Information" school of thought, which came into vogue immediately following World War II, is more modern than the Puritan Ethics School. There are probably salesmen reading these words who can remember the great flurry to "build a better mouse trap," and the company sales meetings, which were devoted almost entirely to product information, tours through the plant, product comparisons with competition, etc. Unfortunately, some of you haven't changed in the past 25 years! You're still telling the prospect how to operate the product *before* you tell him how his problems can be solved.

Today, product features are not as important as they once were. Very frankly, based only on product features, I don't much care whether I buy your product or your competitor's product. There's not that much difference. There can't be. It's impossible for your competitor to stay in business if he markets a product decidedly inferior to yours. Prospects don't really give a hang about product features. What they do want is someone like you to romance them, to warm them with personal interest and concern over problems and needs that are uniquely theirs.

However, the Product–Information School has made a significant contribution to salesmanship. Today's salesman must be well-informed about his product—but not as a first–priority item.

Referring to Diagram 2.2, you will observe that the product takes center-stage-front. The salesman is now relegated to a secondary role, as is the prospect. How well does the Product–Information salesman sell? If you evolved from this school, you may be troubled by the nagging feeling that something is missing in your technique, for the Product–Information salesman characteristically talks 80% of the time, allows the prospect only 20% of the action and closes successfully only 20% of the time.

Perhaps you have perceived on emerging pattern. In the two sales schools that we have reviewed thus far, there seems to be a direct relationship between the amount of time the prospect talks in the presentation and the close ratio. Let's see if this is borne out in the following sales schools.

Let's advance to the next step.

Learn to Avoid the Inadequacies of Scientific Selling

DIAGRAM 2.3

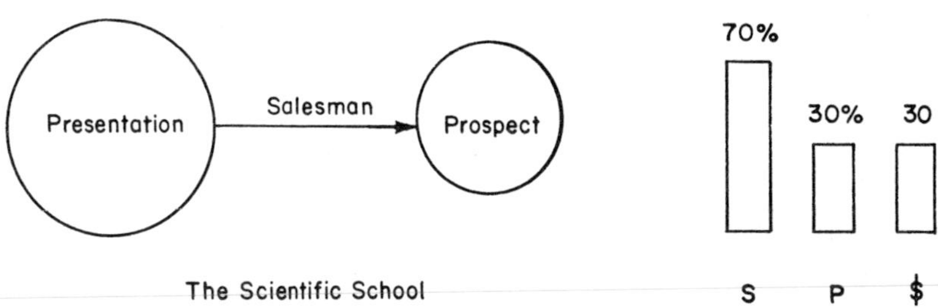

In the early 1950's, as products rapidly improved to a point where making more product-feature differentials proved to be economically unsound, a group of sales managers and trainers got together and reasoned, "There must be something missing. How can we account for the fact that 80% of our salesman are just selling enough to pay their way, but 20% of our salesmen account for the greater part of each of our companies' sales?" This was good reasoning; and this is what they did about it:

They analyzed the many aspects of the sales contact. They looked at the good salesmen and at the poor performers and could see no great differences in outward appearances. Then, the sales presentations were recorded and analyzed and, suddenly, the solution seemed to become obvious. *The words that are used and how they are used*—herein must lie the difference.

Each product was analyzed in relation to the market. Certain features were chosen and converted into the benefits that market surveys reported were important to large clusters of prospects. Further research was made on the "good" presentations. What did they have in common? Can we develop a formula for the "perfect" sales presentation? Yes, it appeared that a standardized sales presentation was possible. The AIDA formula was adopted and heralded as a major breakthrough in sales programs.

Sales managers throughout the country became enthusiastic about the promise of Scientific Selling. All promotion products were encased in the AIDA structure, and the presentations were usually written by a member of the home office sales department with the advice of a committee. The presentations were so highly structured that the prospect spoke only on cue.

The standard presentations were made official, printed and distributed to all members of the sales force. The training meetings that were conducted would more aptly be called "memory courses." Some companies required their salesmen to give each presentation word-for-word. Where there was reluctance to depart from old methods, sales managers enforced the use of the standard, formulated presentation.

We tried to identify words that had a special appeal to prospects. One such word was "new": It became so overused that the poor prospect must have reflected that every product in the catalog was new! We spoke of the inventory of an item as "half–gone" instead of "you still have half your inventory." We inflected voices and repeated phrases for emphasis. We drilled on body position, hand gestures—all in the interests of science!

Was it worthwhile? Were there elements of good, along with the bad? Yes, an important advance was made: the analysis of prospects and sales presentations. Had we known then what we know how, i.e., that all prospects are different and that we must make individual analyses, not mass analyses, the results would have been quite impressive. Nevertheless, sales did advance along with our knowledge of how sales were made.

The sales presentation that some of you are using at this time may not be very different from the formula presentation. Instead of your company doing the analysis, you have, perhaps, unconsciously conducted your own informal study. You may have found the approach that works well for you, how you can best answer a tough objection, and a "feeling" for when and how you can best make a close. Having made certain assumptions about why a prospect should buy a particular item, through your "filter of experience," you have probably developed a fairly automated sales presentation that, give or take a few words and phrases, is much the same regardless of to whom it is being given.

If this is the case, you will be interested in the results that can be achieved with this method. Refer to Diagram 2.3. You will notice that the emphasis has now shifted to the *presentation* as the most important element in the sale. Because the Scientific School believes in prospect participation (although it is rigidly controlled), the prospect speaks about 30% of the total time. Importantly, our pattern of prospect participation/close ratio, previously only hinted at, seems to be pretty well confirmed. This relationship suggests further study.

You Are on the Brink of an Exciting Discovery

We have just reviewed the evolution of salesmanship. If you were honest with yourself, you probably saw yourself moving through these various stages as you grew into the salesman you are today. Whether we speak of a body of knowledge, a culture, an economic system or a person's individual development, we find a gradual shifting of emphasis from one viewpoint and activity to another, as a man or an institution develops in stature and character.

Charles A. Reich, in his book *The Greening of America,** speaks of the development of our national character through similar stages: The hero of our new land in the past century was not worldly, but he possessed the ordinary virtues of plainness, honesty and hard work (Puritan Ethics School). Then he saw "invention and machinery and production [as] the equivalent of progress" and "competition [as] the law of nature and man" (Product–Information School). Then he maintained "that all activities should be carried on in that manner which is scientifically or technically best and most efficient" (Scientific School). Professor Reich states that these beliefs—these elements we have developed as a consequence of our experiences—are "drastically at variance with reality."

You can doubtlessly think of other parallels that further support this development sequence. The important lesson to be learned is that, if we are vital individuals and growing in skill and under-

* Charles A. Reich, *The Greening of America* (New York: Random House, 1970), pp. 24–29.

standing as we progress through life, we are constantly engaged in weighing, sorting out, adapting and rejecting concepts. The basis upon which we make these judgments is often faulty, because our viewpoint is often too narrow, or "drastically at variance with reality."

Let's conduct an experiment to prove this point. Without reading further into the next paragraph, re-read the descriptions of the three schools of salesmanship on the preceding pages. As you read, try to find a characteristic or failing that all three schools have in common. Start your review now and then return to this page.

All three of these schools have a common characteristic. In each, the prospect has been relegated to an unimportant role. He is virtually a bystander in the sales drama. Also, you may have observed that the salesman and the prospect play the roles of opponents. Now I ask you, is this relationship in harmony with reality? Considering that the prospect always plays the role of hero (because he alone can say "Yes"), are we giving him enough good lines? Is the sales play weak because he is being upstaged by the salesman, the product and the presentation?

Turning to your sales technique, how many of the mannerisms of the Puritan Ethic School have you retained out of your mistaken belief that they were in harmony with reality? Many salesmen with whom I have worked religiously believe that *talk* is their stock in trade. Do you? How about "being forceful"? (The prospect calls it "pushy.") Secondly, the Product–Information School has its faithful followers because this is the way most companies have taught their salesmen to behave. They claim, "If the product has 15 features, give 'em the whole load." Modern research has shown that most prospects who buy don't give a darn about 14 of them! Have you burdened your sales story with too much garbage? Lastly, is your sales presentation woefully out-of-date because you have unconsciously fallen into a mechanical patter that you give to all prospects?

Honestly now, where do the deficiencies lie? You may feel that you are not selling at near-potential. Too often, we shun reality and allow our sales consciousness to become the repository and the supporter of sales myths. At this time, it will be difficult to decide to change and "fly right," because I haven't given you any substitute for the sales habits so firmly embedded in your consciousness. I will soon remedy that, but first I want to remind you of something I said earlier.

Much Sales Performance Is Largely Wasteful Because It Is Not Purposeful

Most of the concepts that are "hangers-on" from one or more of the three sales schools—those I have labeled "sales myths"—are out of touch with reality, holding you back from the realization of your full potential and causing you to be wasteful in your sales activities, because they are not purposeful.

Too many companies and too many salesmen have limited themselves by using techniques that may have made solid contributions in the past, but are proving themselves relatively ineffective in the realities of today's fast and affluent marketplace.

Sell More and Easier—the Synergistic Way

Some years ago, a new world of selling was born based on research done in the field of behavioral science in industry. A new psychological school emerged which studied why people act as they do. The behavioral sciences were first directed toward studies of how people work in organizations and, just as importantly, why they do not. It was found that many of the principles had unique applications to selling. Throughout the past few years, a behavioral–science approach to selling has evolved. It has been used in such companies as Pratt Whitney, Blue Cross-Blue Shield and Carborundum Company with striking success.

DIAGRAM 2.4

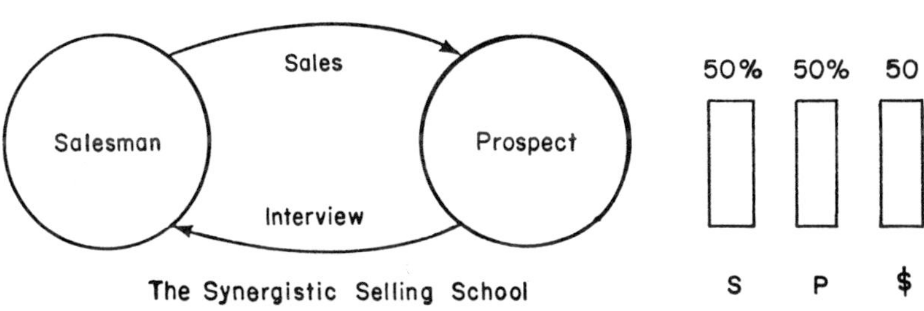

The Synergistic Selling School

Synergistic means "working with" (sin' er jis' tik: *syn* = with + *ergo* = work). In Synergistic Selling, the salesman and the prospect are not opponents; rather, they are members of a team. In working together toward a common goal, the results achieved are greater than the sum of their individual efforts.

Please observe several important characteristics of Diagram 2.4:

1. Neither the salesman nor the prospect plays a subordinate role.
2. Communication is not primarily uni-directional, but is essentially "two-way." The result is not a sales "presentation" but, instead, an "interview."
3. The prospect and the salesman share approximately equal time for expression during the interview.
4. The effectiveness of this technique follows the pattern established in other schools and emphasizes the importance of prospect participation.

Let me now reassure you, Synergistic Selling *will not necessitate a major change in technique*. It is based on what you already know. It is easier than anything you've done before because you'll sell more with less effort. The biggest changes will not be in sales technique but in how you look at selling—your attitude toward your prospects. You'll tell me that what I'm advocating is something you've done for years, but that you have never practiced it to the extent I suggest. It's so simple, you'll wonder why you haven't used it more extensively in the past.

Here are the premises on which Synergistic Selling is based:

1. Every prospect has built-in "motivators" or human needs. They are not "created" by the salesman, but exist in the individual as a result of his heredity, his attitudes, his environment, his life's experiences.
2. These motivators will surface and attach themselves to any product or service that can be translated by the salesman into *value* to the prospect. The way to create value is through interacting—allowing the prospect to enter into the sales talk, to become a part of it, to participate. That's why I call it a *sales interview,* not a sales presentation.

3. Selling is not a salesman-oriented experience; nor is it a prospect-oriented experience. It is a balance, an interacting, a "doing-together" experience. It is not a presentation of product facts on the one hand, nor the subjection of the salesman to the moods and attitudes of the prospect on the other. It is a sharing experience.
4. In order for the salesman to initiate this synergism he needs:
   a. All the information he can secure concerning the prospect, not to form opinions or make judgments, but to be able to prestructure the sales interview to uncover the hidden motivators.
   b. A fine sense of social perception. This is similar to empathy—a "feeling for"—yet it has a broader connotation. Social perception means identifying the needs, the aspirations, the beliefs and attitudes of the prospect. Again, the salesman must keep an open mind to be sensitive, to perceive but not to prejudice his attitudes toward the prospect by judging or classifying him.

Synergistic Selling is the fourth school of salesmanship. It is today's school, in intimate touch with today's reality. Today's prospect is better educated, more knowledgeable, more wanting of ego-satisfying products and buying experiences. Synergistic Selling is "selling with him" toward a common goal: his need satisfaction. It embraces all of the Dynamic Laws that we have found, not only in the laboratory but also in the marketplace. The Dynamic Laws are important in getting him to participate in the sales interview, to reveal his needs, wants and problems so that he can use his own motivation to buy.

DURING THE NEXT WEEK . . .

Focus on your performance in dealing with the prospect. Are you the kind of salesman *you'd* buy from if the roles were reversed?

1. The hardest thing in the world is to be completely honest with yourself. Where do you stand on the quality of your sales interview?

2. Much sales performance is wasteful because it is not purposeful. What is your purpose in a sales interview? Is it to sell him something? To satisfy a want? To solve a problem?
3. Sales effectiveness follows a pattern in direct proportion to the amount of time a prospect is permitted to talk. Do you do all the talking from the mistaken belief you have a limited time to "get all your licks in"?
4. Today, there is little difference between products. Are you the kind of salesman who offers a differential in yourself?
5. Most sales presentations today are automated presentations. Are you fearful of breaking with a standard sales patter and allowing the interview to zero-in on target?
6. Many sales presentations are out of touch with reality. Are you using yesterday's sales techniques on today's customers?
7. Sales habits of another day are really sales myths. Are you wasting precious calls and precious years by clinging to them?
8. I have promised you more sales, easier sales, through the simple expedient of involving the prospect. Will you open your mind to new techniques and develop synergistic relationships with your prospects in order to sell better?
9. Every prospect has built-in motivators or human needs. Are you willing to explore the simple techniques to get him to reveal his wants and his needs?
10. The way to create value for your product is through interaction with the prospect. Do not be averse to a new, more exciting way to sell.
11. A salesman must learn all he can about a prospect and develop a keen sense of perception. This is the homework, but it will become second nature in time.

3

How to Use the Prospect's Own Momentum to Sell More

The ways in which we sell today seem natural and inevitable. They evolved as did most of our business practices, based on what seemed to be sufficient evidence at that time.

Had the information contained in this chapter been available 50 years ago, you might very well be selling in quite a different way and living a more satisfying and rewarding life as a salesman.

Develop the Prospect's Will to Buy

There are some salesmen who believe that the only motivation needed to get the order is a friendly smile, a firm handshake, a salesman-controlled sales presentation, a quick, forceful answer to an objection and a persuasive close. Perhaps this was enough when sales quotas were low and salesmen's needs were modest. But when you want to *improve* sales and get more satisfaction, advancement and money from sales work, you must learn how to develop *your prospect's will to buy.*

Early research in the complex salesman-prospect interaction seemed to suggest that the salesman who was warm and friendly performed better than the salesman who centered his attention on the prospect and the task to be done. More recent and exacting research studies have disproved this common myth and pointed toward more detailed analysis and investigation of the prospect as the key to unlocking more sales doors.

The truth is that we are not involving prospects at their full capacity in the sales process. We are not permitting them to make as great a contribution as they can to the successful outcome of the sale. Specifically, the usual sales presentations take advantage of only the minimal performance that prospects are capable of. Traditionally, the salesman appeals to product features to motivate the prospect and the prospect has little or no opportunity to signal his higher psychological needs. The result is that the salesman finds himself working harder and longer to accomplish less and less in terms of sales production.

Because we make eight or ten or more sales encounters during a sales day and repeat the routine five days a week for 50 weeks in a year, the sales presentation tends to become automated. Although we can automate a sales talk, we cannot automate human nature. And that's the rub.

The human needs of prospects are the pivot-point of any effective sales interview. They must become the *floor* on which a sales talk is built. Oversimplified, this means you must allow the prospect to talk. Later I will tell you how you can do this and still stay in control. He must talk because he'll tell you, in response to the proper questions, *how he can be sold!* The salesman then points his product presentation toward the needs the prospect has revealed. Once the prospect sees a match between his needs and your product, you have developed his will to buy.

Motivation vs. Stimulation

There exists a great deal of confusion over the term "motivation." To most, *motivation* is synonymous with *stimulation*. We commonly say of an inspiring speech that it was "motivating," when we really mean "stimulating." There's an important difference. You can stimulate with a speech or a kick in the pants, but the effect soon evaporates. Motivation, which makes contact with inner wants, needs and desires, is more powerful, more permanent and results in action

All behavior, including buying behavior, is motivated. For a prospect to buy from you, he must be motivated, i.e., he must sense that certain needs can be fulfilled or problems solved by taking the action you suggest. When he doesn't buy, this too is an action or decision that is motivated. Thus, prospects have positive and negative motives when viewed from your position. A positive motive might be the trust and rapport you build up by helping the prospect make a contribution to his company's profit objectives. For example, negative motives, which result in a "No" decision, might be a salesman's evasions, irrelevancies, objections and other defensive maneuvers during his sales talk.

Strictly speaking, one cannot motivate another; a motive is an internalized entity. It is the result of a lifetime of living: of family life, experiences with people, jobs and situations, education. A motive, as with an opinion, may have been formed early in a person's life or it may be the result of a recent experience. A market researcher may say that "there is a substantial demand" for a *green* Dingywampus in the market. But as you make your sales rounds, you don't know for sure that a given prospect truly wants a green Dingywampus. So you allow him to participate in a mental exploration to uncover his own unique problems and needs. Once these have been identified, you are in a strong position to show him why the green Dingywampus is just the thing to solve that problem, to fill that need. Remember, however, that the motive already existed. You didn't create it; it surfaced as a result of your questions, which compelled the prospect to think, to uncover, to bring forth the idea.

In selling, you have only half of the puzzle: the product, or satisfier. The prospect has the other half: the need, or problem. Sales motivation is a subtle process of getting him to reveal the need or problem through his participation in the interview and showing him how the need can be fulfilled with your product.

The Prospect Decides in Ways That Make Sense to Him

Occasionally, a salesman will say, "I can't understand why he didn't buy. He has a need for my product." Of course he didn't buy! The salesman made the assessment of need, not the prospect. Apparently, the prospect saw no need that could be fulfilled through buying. Far too often we make the decision and forget that it is the prospect's prerogative to decide. This is muddy thinking. Also, what do we mean by "need"? Don't we mean that the prospect could probably "buy" or "use" the product? Good selling starts with good thinking. As was mentioned earlier: Selling is a mental activity. And precise thinking is a must if we are to understand and make full use of the Dynamic Laws.

As the prospect makes the decision, surely it's only prudent to turn our attention to him and examine the sales contact from his vantage point.

The prospect (along with all of us!) is constantly seeking ways to enhance his self-image. Studies in social psychology demonstrate that approximately 80% of the time a businessman spends in thinking (about anything other than his work), he spends in thinking about himself. More specifically, he concerns himself with what psychologists call his "level of expectations." His level might include many things: the position in the business hierarchy at which he hopes to arrive; what he hopes to acquire in material possessions; how he would like his associates and friends to regard him; what strategies and plans he'll employ to achieve his goals. We will examine these expectations in detail in Chapter 4.

If you want to understand what motivates a man—a prospect, a friend or a family member—you can gain valuable insight into his complex nature by understanding his expectations of himself and his expectations of his environment. A salesman who does not understand his prospect is one who can see no point of view other than his own. He deals in generalities and assumes, for example, that all people are motivated by money simply because he himself is motivated by money. Thus, he automates his sales presentation and handles all prospects as if they were much the same, and in so doing, never allows the prospect to participate and contribute to his success.

On the temple of Delphi, high on the hills of Greece, is inscribed, *From the gods comes the saying "Know thyself."* As you examine the Dynamic Laws, you will have the opportunity to know yourself a little better—to understand your basic motivations. In learning more about yourself, you can avoid the projection of your own value systems into the behavior of your prospect.

At this point you may question, with justification, if it is realistic to turn your back on rational considerations such as price, availability, service, etc., in an effort to explore ego motivations. It is not my intention to avoid rational considerations; instead, it is to open a new door to buying motivation which you might not have used before. Later in this chapter, rational and emotional motivations will be brought into proper perspective.

Several months ago, I was discussing this same subject with the Chief Purchasing Agent of a medical supply firm. He expressed the relationship between the hard, rational approach and the more subtle, self-image approach so well, I jotted down his comment. "When the salesman is finished," he said, "I do a mental summation, which might go like this: 'Well OK, the Profit Income is good. Now I'll add up my Psychic Income—the income of the spirit.' Usually all the salesman gives me is Profit Income. The man who walks away with the order is the one who gives me Psychic Income as well."

The buying motivation we must uncover dwells in the prospect. He may decide in peculiar ways, but they are ways that make sense to him. And that's why you can't make generalizations based on your experience or that of a thousand market researchers. The Kendall Company, makers of diapers (among many other splendid products), found this out. For years, their sales appeals were directed toward what their diapers would do for baby. There was only mild interest. Now they tell mother what the product will do for her. "She broke the doors down to buy," says Kendall's President, John L. McCanchie.

The reasons people buy are highly individualized and infinitely more numerous than all the product features you could possibly present. Thus, by changing your presentation sequence from *product feature-prospect need* to *prospect need-product feature,* you will broaden the sales appeal of your product. You can appeal to *more* prospects in *more* ways than ever before—and *each time you will be on the right track*. You're talking about a human need—not *any* human need, but *his* need—and that is infinitely more exciting (motivating!) than anything you can do.

What Makes Anybody a Prospect?

In the vast literature that has accumulated in the 50 years or so that research has studied why people behave in the ways they do, one fact stands out as consistent and unchanging: Man is a goal-striving organism. He has goals, wants, needs, desires. He has two images: one his *true* self, as he sees himself in more candid moments, and the other his *would-be* self, the image he is constantly projecting to the people in his environment. As soon as he satisfies one need, another emerges to take its place—all in an effort to enhance his image.

In a sense, he is always a prospect until his dying day because his needs never quit. He is always reaching out and stretching to advance to a level higher than his present circumstances.

The limiting factor in selling is never the prospect. The limitations are of our own doing, and those over which we have full control. There is the limitation of product; however, this is not usually a serious limitation because we can easily modify, change and upgrade products, and we can almost never saturate a market. The major limitation exists in our inability to probe for the inner drives, motives, and needs that bring the realization to the mind of a prospect that here is a product that will help him achieve his goal. This is what motivation is all about.

Everyone you encounter has these motives. That's why everybody and anybody can be a prospect.

Your Use of the Dynamic Laws Can Help Overcome Major Obstacles

I needn't recount the full range of sales obstacles to you (you know them only too well), but here are a few:

- The tough prospect who wants to play a game to see how insulting he can be.
- The perennial stand off: "Your price is too high."
- The problem of a friendship or family relationship with a favored competitor.
- The call-back problem: Someone can't make up his mind; or is it the "run-around"?

There are also some relatively new problems:

- Committee buying
- Standardized buying
- Home office buying
- Approval buying

These are all difficult problems, some seemingly without a clear solution. Prospect-participation selling will not solve all of them; but the intelligent use of the Dynamic Laws will put you a lot closer to scoring a breakthrough than any method you have used thus far.

I personally have found the Dynamic Laws of great practical value in my selling against obstacles; and the reason they work is quite simple: The greatest sales force on earth is *the power of self interest.* A buyer can lean back on specs ("It hasn't been approved for buying" and "I have to refer it to the buying committee") all he wants to, but as soon as you have uncovered the pot of self interest and he sees a match between your product and his wants, you're well on the way to success. He'll find a way to speed up the process, to circumvent it or to make an exception.

Keep in mind, of course, that the prospect will weigh his alternatives. If achieving his personal goal isn't worth the criticism, the inconvenience or the time involved, he may remain inactive. Each prospect has his own values. Also, most prospects behave the way they do because this is the way we (and countless other salesmen) have taught them to behave. Their behavior during the sales talk is the product of many sales presentations—some bad, some good, a very few excellent. Prospects stall, raise objections, evade the issue, argue and effectively use silence, because they have been made to feel threatened by many salesmen. Furthermore, these reactions become firmly established as habits by the traditional methods employed by most salesmen in trying to combat such a prospect (hard questions, exaggeration, argument and pressure). The next time you experience a major sales trauma, the chances are excellent that you can chalk it up to a salesman who thought he was on a one-way street with the prospect and had a dilly of a head-on collision!

Look For The Prospect's Feelings—They're More Important Than Rational Considerations

As much as we try to sell "logically," selling is not a logical process. Remember the old saying: "One man manufactured something everybody needed. He made a living. Another manufactured something nobody needed but everybody wanted. He made a fortune."

One might *logically* argue, "One must eat to live." This is perfectly *rational.* But what follows in our affluent society: a bowl of rice or a T-bone steak with baked potato, tossed salad, etc.? What lies between a handful of rice and a juicy steak is how you *feel* about it.

Time Magazine reported that the average urban family spends only 48.7% of its after-tax income on food, shelter and clothing. Thus, it has 51.3% left over to spend as it pleases. The percentage of discretionary income is actually greater than 51.3% when you consider that the average urban family stuffs itself with a too-rich diet, lives in a $22,500 home and buys "name-brand" clothing. The average family is free to spend the greater part of its income as it "feels like it." And it does—in gratification of its psychological wants.

Are there exceptions to this generalization? Yes, indeed. If you're selling construction materials or labor, heavy equipment, etc., "the lowest price gets the contract." The engineer keeps telling you that "all I'm interested in are the specs and the price." Well . . . maybe. Is the engineer really interested in only specs and price? Or is he much like the rest of us? Let's see. This morning the engineer's young son spit out his Pablum the same way yours did; his wife got the bank balance overdrawn, same as yours; he uttered an unbecoming oath when told his mother-in-law was coming for a visit. It's a mistake to regard the engineer (or anyone) as an automaton. He's human. He has basic needs that facts alone do not satisfy.

Usually, selling is a very personal interaction of prospect and salesman. Think for a minute of your best customer—the one who buys more from you than any other customer. To what do you attribute your success with him: your personality or your product? Without a doubt, it is your personality. When the prospect likes the salesman, the entire relationship between prospect and salesman—including communication and behavior—is favorable to the completion of the sale. This relationship that you develop is the result of your ability to make contact with the status and ego needs of the buyer—to help him feel important—to afford recognition of his accomplishments.

Look toward the human side of selling: the social wants, the ego-drives. They exist even in those situations where big business has tried to de-humanize selling in the interests of efficiency. Satisfy the rational requirements as best you can (as will your competitor) and then add the "plus" that your competitor can't: look for the human elements that exist in the feelings and emotions of the buyer.

Herbert A. Simon said it well:

> It is impossible for the behavior of a single isolated individual to reach any degree of rationality. . . . Even an approximation of objective rationality is hard to conceive.*

Go That Extra Distance to Success

We are ready now to bring the relationship between rational requirements and emotional requirements into perspective. To understand this relationship would be to make great progress toward understanding the Dynamic Laws of Motivation and using these laws to improve sales performance.

Dr. Frederick Herzberg ** has contributed substantially to our understanding of motivation with his explanation of the relationship between rational needs (which he calls Hygiene Factors) and emotional wants (which he calls Motivation Factors).

MOTIVATION AND HYGIENE FACTORS

Motivation Factors	Ego Needs Social Needs Salesman's Ability to Relate
Hygiene Factors	Product Features, Price, Availability, Delivery, Installation, Maintenance Warranty, Research, Location, Credit, etc.

DIAGRAM 3-1

* Herbert A. Simon, *Administrative Behavior* (New York, N.Y.: The Macmillan Co., 1961.)

** Frederick Herzberg, "One More Time: How Do You Motivate Employees?" (Harvard Business Review, Volume 46, Number 1, 1968) p. 57.

Diagram 3-1 is to be interpreted in this way: Certain Hygiene Factors must be present in any sales situation for a sale to be consummated. But these factors *do not in themselves* bring about the sale. In other words, certain rational or hygiene factors must be satisfied as a prerequisite to the sale. Such factors might be one or more necessary product features, a certain price range, availability of the product and reasonable delivery, etc. A *negative* influence for successful completion of the sale may exist if certain rational needs important to the prospect are not present; however the presence of all important rational needs does not necessarily constitute a *positive* influence on the sale. If all rational requirements are met, successful completion of the sale is then dependent on the motivational factors.

The Rational-Hygiene Factors may be thought of as the *floor* on which we, as salesmen, build the sales interview. They are the price of admission, not the show itself. These factors usually do not constitute a problem because they are usually present—they have to be for a company to stay in business. It is for this reason that, in our highly competitive business world, there is little real difference between Product A and Product B. The real difference exists in *you*—the salesman—in your ability to relate to the customer's ego and social wants. This is where true motivation exists—it's all "above the line."

The Emotional-Motivation Factors area is your domain—where you, through the adroit use of investigation, observation, questions and problem definition, uncover the emotional needs of the prospect that move him to buy.

Empathy Means Money In The Bank For You

To understand a prospect's motivation, we must look at his environment the way he does. To do this requires a rather rare quality in anyone—especially a salesman. This quality is known as empathy. It is the ability to project yourself mentally into the other person's spirit: to walk in his shoes, to sit behind his desk, to be subject to all the daily pressures and pleasures that he experiences. You see, we all look out at the world through a window—a window colored by our experiences, hopes and disappointments.

Don't confuse empathy with sympathy. Empathy is a "feeling with." Sympathy is a "feeling for."

This is a particularly critical area for a salesman. Not only is it important for him to develop this quality if he is to sell big, but it is especially difficult for him to do so because of his personality. The best salesmen I know are ego-centered. Don't be offended; this is simply our common personality characteristic. Being egoistic, it's hard to shift our focus to the other fellow; yet we must if we are to understand his viewpoint and how he sees our product in relation to his motivation.

Motivation is not simply what you say or do as a salesman to influence your prospect. People are motivated to buy when they recognize a "psychological advantage" to themselves. The various internal forces that influence the prospect's viewpoint and, hence, contribute toward his recognition or rejection of psychological advantage are illustrated in Diagram 3-2, the Frame–of–Reference Chart.*

Do you begin to see how a canned sales presentation or an automatic presentation simply can't be effective? We lose too many prospects because we can't demonstrate psychological advantage to them.

Don't try to memorize the chart in Diagram 3-2. It's too complicated to try to remember; but be conscious of the many factors that influence a prospect's viewpoint. The process we shall follow to determine the prospect's motive is very simple.

A prospect will make a buying decision measured against this Frame of Reference or viewpoint. Thus, his Frame of Reference becomes a subconscious "filter" by which a proposed course of action is judged. When a particular action, judged against this standard, seems to make the prospect appear to be small and unworthy, he'll reject it. On the other hand, he is motivated to buy when the proposed action seems to promise him that he'll feel bigger—the man he wants to be.

How to Apply Motivation to Your Sales Interview

Uncover Problems

Every day, each one of us lives with problems that cry out for solutions. True, we give them little time or attention until a crisis

---

* Reprinted by permission from *Sales Management, The Marketing Magazine.* Copyright, 1967.

DIAGRAM 3.2

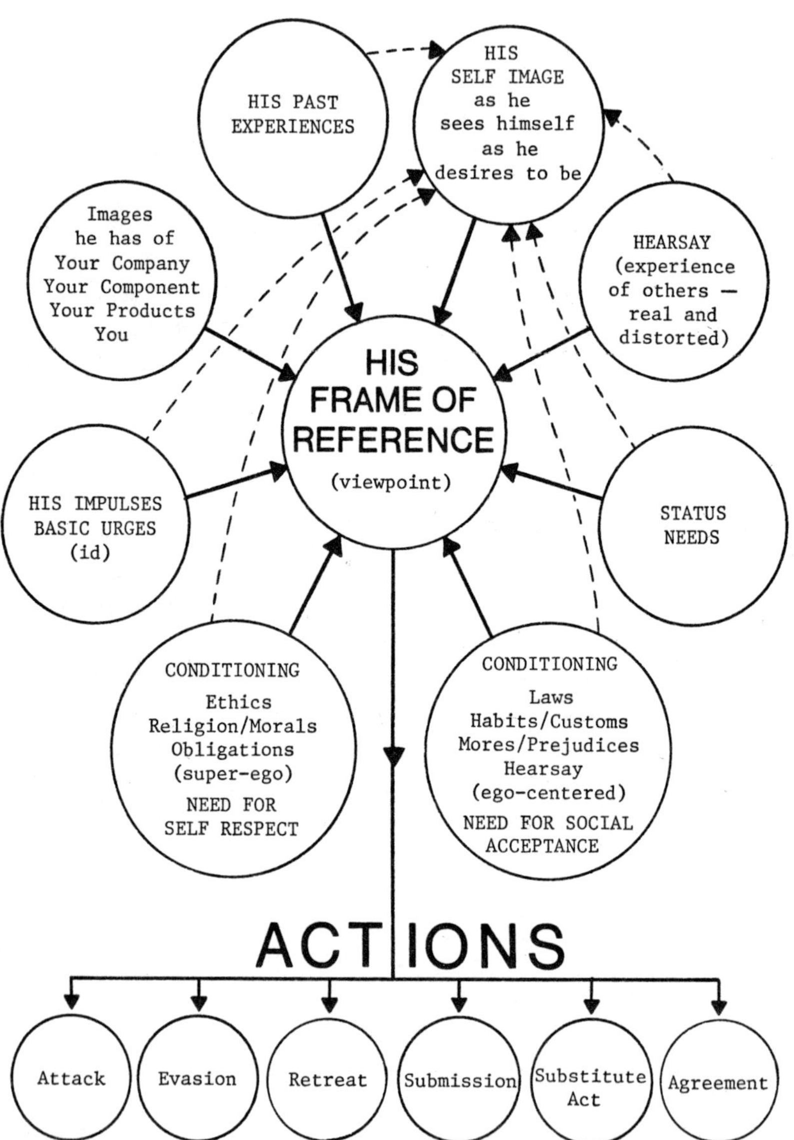

FRAME-OF-REFERENCE CHART: A man will usually act from his own frame of reference, a way of seeing things that is conditioned by many things: status needs, past experiences, and so on. Most important of these, however, is his self image, which changes as he matures and grows.

develops. Then the problems surface and we want immediate action. What are your chances of calling on such a prospect just at that specific time? Almost nil. Replacement trucks for a fleet are purchased every two or three years. Typewriters in an office, about every five years. A new home, maybe every seven years. Are these people prospects *only* at these times? No! Each has problms. Don't sell a product; sell an idea—sell a solution. Probe for hidden problems and motivations. Show a prospect how a problem that hasn't reached the hot point of crisis can be overcome now. Then, with competition calls two years down the line, there will be no problem, because you have exercised empathy.

Prospecting

Use your imagination. What psychological as well as economic needs will your product fulfill? Next, look at your product from the buyer's viewpoint. What new prospects can you find as a result? A real estate salesman saw, as did everyone in the east end of Lincolnville, the slow but relentless encroachment of a shopping center on a fairly nice residential area. He empathized that some home owners saw their psychic need for status and prestige being violated by the shopping center. He sold them new homes, got a good price for their old ones and resold them to small business owners. Three commissions on each! Did anyone call him to tell him they had a problem? No. But he knew people and uncovered the hidden revolt to the noise and traffic of the large stores.

Dairies once struggled with large, heavy glass milk bottles that often broke, until an enterprising paper salesman looked at the buyer's Frame of Reference and developed paper cartons. A multimillion dollar business—all from the practice of empathy!

Approach

Jim Biggs had been selling typewriters for three years. His egocentered approach step was similar to this: "Need a new typewriter? Let me tell you about this one." Nobody *needed* a new typewriter, but they needed expert help in office design, in decreasing maintenance costs. Now he motivates prospects with "Would you be interested in how you can save up to 25% in rent?" Understand the inner drives of people; look for potential problems—but *from the buyer's point of view.* Talk systems design, improved methods, increased effectiveness—this is what prospects want to hear. Anybody can sell a typewriter; few can sell a need.

Benefits

Don't waste your breath telling prospects how a product works. They won't listen anyway, until you make contact with needs, wants and desires. When they buy the idea that a want can be satisfied, they'll want to know how to operate the product. Until then, they don't care. This doesn't mean that product information is not important—but it means it's in second place. It's a Hygiene Factor until the prospect recognizes that he can live better, feel better, save money, gain prestige, advance socially, be secure, etc. Then he can't wait to get his hands on it!

Objections

Older methods of salesmanship taught the prospect how to object, stall or make excuses, because salesmen didn't allow him to talk and to reveal his inner needs. The salesmen did all the talking; they "controlled" the conversation; they threatened him. You can't remake history, but you can resolve next time to probe the prospect's psychic wants. That's his favorite subject; he won't object to his brainchild. He takes the venom out of his objection and it becomes a simple question.

Close

An insurance salesman called on me several days ago. (I never turn down a salesman. I learn much from each.) By using questions, he invited me to talk the greater part of the time. My answers were precise and to the point. He very easily closed with the question, "I can see you are a man used to making decisions. May I expect a decision from you in three days?" He found my motive, a characteristic I take pride in: My ability to make rapid decisions! He looked at his product through my window.

Why the Dynamic Laws Make Sense to the Professional

Time after time, following sales seminars given throughout the U.S., I've had men making $50,000 to $100,000 a year come up to me and say "At last, it all makes sense." What they're saying is that their sales life has been an *evolution*. Each day they have learned something they could use to better their performance before the prospect; but they have also been perplexed in their lack of understanding of prospects. "Why do some buy and others, given the same logical arguments, fail to go ahead?" The answer is always found in an analysis of the prospect. Although we'll never know for sure how a prospect will react, these salesmen do me a great honor when they emphasize that a better knowledge of people gives them the basis for inquiry into prospect motivations.

Thus, the material we have covered may seem to fight with some of the notions you have held before and, in a sense, it may be, as professional salesmen point out, somewhat *revolutionary*. Calling it "revolutionary" makes it nonetheless desirable; for after all, the major difference between an evolution and a revolution is simply the speed with which change takes place.

To the beginning salesman, this means you can save valuable time by starting now to apply the Dynamic Laws. After all, time is the stuff of which life is made. Why wait 15 years to arrive at the goals you have set for yourself when two years of studious application of motivational principles will get you there?

If you are an established salesman, start now to look at your customers with a new eye. Review your call reports or prospect calls. If you make notations of prospect reactions (e.g., advertising support appealed to him), you are in a good position to tailor your new presentation so that it will satisfy a need already proven to be important. If you don't make notations of prospect reactions, start now. For example, if your customer is learning how to promote his business, appeal to his ability to display and advertise. Is he trying to develop new skills, new abilities? Through the medium of your product, can you show him that his skills and abilities can be developed? He, like you, is constantly changing. Is he acquiring new knowledge? Greater maturity? If so, how can your service and product fit into his plan? Remember that taking a prospect for granted and not matching his progress with new opportunities and new challenges is a good way to lose him.

Admittedly, we are dealing with many variables: the product variable—some products do not exhibit a high propensity for social and ego gratification; the prospect variable—people are highly individualized; the motivation variable—needs vary in substance as well as degree.

Obviously, if prospects were all stamped out of the same mold and lived in a strictly controlled laboratory environment, subject to uniform stimuli, there would be no variables—and no salesmen. Knowing that all prospects would react in the same manner, the company could merely send out a letter and order blank at predetermined times of the year. The company could even predict results precisely. This will never be the case. The salesman requires the ability to interact with the prospect—a skill, unfortunately, that is in very short supply.

Despite these variables, if people can see the fulfillment of one or more of their wants, they will be motivated to act to a degree never before imagined by the salesman who has heretofore never realized the importance people attach to their psychic needs. They, too, want challenges, rewards and a way to achieve goals.

4

How to Work the Four Basic Laws of Human Motivation in Selling Dynamically

People rarely buy on product needs alone. Yet most sales presentations are built on a discussion of product. All things being equal, most buying is strongly influenced by inner personality needs. This fact, when accepted and acted upon, presents many new opportunities to you to convert many poor prospects to consistent customers.

Look for the Differences That Count

Most of us do a great deal of generalizing. This is not surprising; it is simply the way we have been taught since early childhood. Much of man's intellectual progress is a direct result of the ordering or categorizing of facts. Charles Darwin once said, "Science consists of grouping facts so that general laws or conclusions may be drawn from them."

A characteristic of physical science is that results are predictable (and this is a generalization in itself). However, although certain aspects of human behavior are predictable, we handicap ourselves unnecessarily when we apply generalizations to our consideration of an *individual* prospect's needs and desires. A tire salesman may reflect on the fact that he sells more tires on those days his company advertises a weekend special. He generalizes, "Customers are primarily interested in low price." With this generalization controlling his presentation, he tries to sell Mr. Brown a new set of tires by emphasizing low price; however, Mr. Brown, using his own generalization, equates low price with inferior quality and is not persuaded to buy. Had the salesman pursued a plan to first identify Mr. Brown's motivation as one of safety and then appealed to this need, the outcome may have been successful.

We all have a tendency to arrange prospect characteristics into categories. In so doing, *we escape reality!* Thus, we say in defense: "The guy's a cheapskate," "He's belligerent," "He's a chronic objector," etc., when in reality he is none of these things. In reality, we didn't get to know him at all. There's nothing wrong with categories, as long as we realize that reality can't be categorized!

Part of our problem is that we tend to polarize our thinking. We think of a characteristic as having only two faces—one at one pole and the other at the opposite pole; black or white, friendly or unfriendly, good or bad, etc. A salesman calling on a retail merchant describes the elaborate advertising program that supports his product. The merchant is not impressed. He says he'll switch the customers to his longer-margin item. Two poles, two opposite views, separated by a continuum recognized by neither the salesman nor the merchant. Reality exists somewhere in this continuum. If the salesman resigns himself to this defeat, he comes away with the generalization that the customer was "difficult." If, on the other hand, he looks for differences, he thinks, "How different is his Frame of Reference from mine?" He inquires, "I know you're a good sales person. How many customers out of ten can you switch?" Of course, you know where this question will lead: Any figure the merchant mentions will leave the door open for an order.

Is it any wonder that we jump at generalizations? Somehow, it's easier; it saves time; it orders confusion, even if it isn't true. To the merchant, it gives him a feeling of security—that everything is under control. The salesman, it provides him with an alibi. Again, selling is a *mental* activity. The thinking salesman considers the continuum and inquires as to what the difference is in reality.

If you were an advertising manager, you would be interested in what the market surveys had to say about the advantages prospective customers see in your product. You would write your advertising copy so that it would appeal to the needs held in common by thousands of would-be customers. Here, generalizations are important.

As a salesman, you are probably selling on a one-to-one relationship—you and one prospect. This *one* prospect has to be sold. He doesn't necessarily follow the averages established by the market survey. If you treat him as you would a dozen others (even give him a canned presentation), you are moving away from reality (for you don't know where it exists) and surrendering accuracy for the security of an alibi if the sale is not made.

The trouble is that each individual prospect doesn't fit neatly into a category. What make a person unique are his differences, and finding his differences as well as his similarities. This makes selling a challenging, exciting and rewarding profession. Evaluate each prospect to determine his individual Frame of Reference, his variations from the average, his unique problems, rather than assuming that all prospects are alike and prejudging them from generalizations.

In my book *Synergistic Selling,* it is pointed out:

> Most salesmen can sell a reasonable amount of merchandise by merely telling the story frequently enough. But you won't get rich until you learn to sell when circumstances are not favorable. It's selling in the face of characteristics which are different from the average that is the badge of good salesmanship. When prospects react differently, this difference is their vulnerable spot. It involves their special needs, their self-image, their goals, their problems. Disregard it and you go down in ignoble defeat! The trick is to identify it and make favorable contact with it.*

George Santayana said: "When men and women agree, it is only in their conclusions; their reasons are always different."

This quotation might be phrased in sales terms: "When customers buy, they are similar only in their actions; their reasons are always different."

Focus on the Buyer's Need—That's Where the Action Is

I'm going to ask you to change the way you look at selling for just a moment. *In all reality, the salesman never sells!* What he does is to "condition" the prospect's mind. The prospect buys—

---

* H. B. Rames, *Synergistic Selling* (Lincoln, Neb.: Springboard Associates, 1971), p. 74.

that's the action. Conditioning is a psychological term, which means bringing about a desired response as a result of implied satisfaction of a need. You may recall the experiments of Ivan Pavlov while studying the digestion of dogs. He noted increased salivation when he showed them food.

The salesman *conditions* the prospect when he probes for need and then describes his product in relation to that need. When the prospect sees a match between his need and the salesman's product, this is the *stimulus*. The *response* is a decision to buy. The *action* is signing the order, taking delivery, etc. The sale is made not in the salesman's mind, but in the prospect's mind. This fact underscores the importance of knowing what's going on in the prospect's mind; for that's where the action is. To help us to know what to look for, we need a working knowledge of human behavior—of those needs that motivate buying behavior. This knowledge will not only allow you to sell better; it will improve your sales personality.

The Frame-of-Reference Chart in Chapter 3 makes it amply clear that, with literally hundreds of events and backgrounds influencing a man's outlook on life, each prospect will be quite different from any other. We often call this a "set of values" or say "his value system is different." Thus, a prospect who was reared in poverty will have a different value system than the son of a well-to-do father. For instance, he looks at money differently. He may attach "value" to it out of proportion to the value that the salesman attaches to it. It may mean the "good things in life" to him, but to the rich-son prospect who has always had the "good things in life," money has little value. Security, to one prospect, no matter what his station in life might be at the time, may mean having a good job in a stable business. However, the man with an affluent background might be bored to death in such a job and might be motivated to engage in a risk enterprise.

Such differences are a surprisingly permanent part of an individual's makeup. The prospect with a poverty background will usually have an exaggerated respect for money even if his work has given him unusually high monetary rewards. A salesman can't change such a permanent set of values; but he can identify it (the clues are abundant), make contact with it and sell by stressing the benefits that seem to support the prospect's value system.

Your Role as a Change Agent

Prospects are not, of course, unchangeable. A prospect with whom you may have dealt for years, whose past buying behavior has given you a fertile file of material on which to base his buying motivations, can change from a "nice guy" to a "bad guy" (or the reverse) for no apparent reason. Here, it becomes necessary to resort to generalization to explain this change. Motivations, biases, instincts, attitudes, habits—the whole gamut of factors that determine buying action, may be categorized into two classifications:

1. The Intrinsic Factors: those that are a result of heredity and early childhood experiences; and those that are so extreme that they leave an indelible impression on one's psyche.

2. The Extrinsic or Acquired Factors: those that are formed as a result of one's interaction with one's environment.

The intrinsic factors exert a profound influence on a person's actions throughout life. Some factors may remain dormant for a period of time; but when the prospect is confronted with a strong stimulus (a crisis in life, for instance), the intrinsic factor may surface and take control of his actions.

The acquired or extrinsic factors are more amenable to change. As a man's environment changes, he discovers that certain biases, opinions, etc., no longer work well, and he acquires new and more serviceable ones.

Thus, at any moment, a prospect may react to motivations laid down when he was four years old, or he may react to something as recent as the burnt toast his wife served him for breakfast. The task before you seems to get very complicated. It isn't really; for the methods you use to elicit identity of needs, wants and problems are the same. It's just that you must be aware that one prospect is different from another and that he may be different today from the way he was yesterday.

A man reacts to the acute, short–duration factors of his environment. Thus, a normally placid individual may be short–tempered when fatigued and overworked. (Save your breath. Call on him next week.) A difficult prospect may become friendly when he senses that his inner needs may be fulfilled by accepting your recommendation.

The key to using the Dynamic Laws is found in this knowledge of the prospect. You've known people who, in the words of the poet, can change the whole complexion of a day. You are "an acute factor in the environment" of every prospect you call on. You are an agent of change. When the prospect sees his need of praise, recognition, acceptance, esteem, etc., satisfied by buying, he changes from "not buying" or "buying from your competitor" to buying from you. Don't underestimate the strength of inner personality needs; we all have them in great quantity. This is the heart of motivation.

Let's examine these needs and wants of people so that you'll have the knowledge and background to know what to look for in your sales interview.

The Pyramid of Psychological Needs

Probably the simplest and most widely accepted reference that serves to explain human motivation is the Pyramid of Needs.

Before we proceed to explain each step, bear in mind the two basic concepts on which this philosophy is based:

1. Man is a goal-striving, need-motivated being.
2. He always has unfulfilled needs. As one need is satisfied, another emerges to take its place.

Physiological Needs

This is the most basic motivation: to satisfy the basic needs of food, shelter and clothing. Physiological needs must be satisfied before other needs emerge, because they are concerned with survival. It is generally not an important motivation in America today because of our standard of living; but it is important in some countries (India, for example) where minimum requirements for life are lacking.

Despite the relative unimportance of this need in America, much of our thinking is erroneously based on this motivation. Money is

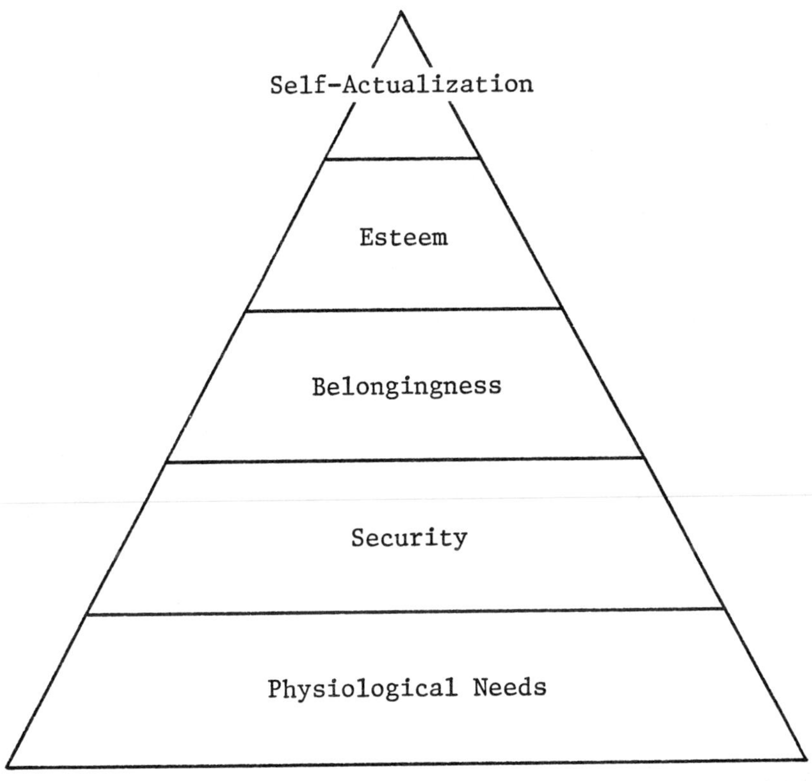

PYRAMID OF NEEDS

somehow confused with providing the necessities of life. Strikes are called because "our salaries are not keeping up with the cost of living index," and the workers drive from their $40,000 homes in their $4,000 cars to carry a sign in the picket line. "We can't buy milk for our children." Man may reason, "I must work to eat," as he sits down to a T-Bone steak dinner.

This is a confusion of rational and emotional needs. In our affluent society, money has little to do with providing for physiological needs. It's what money means in emotional terms that's important. If management were to provide more status and recognition to workers, some "cost of living" strikes might be averted. You as a salesman must look beyond what money and price mean to a prospect. Usually there's a higher need that requires satisfaction;

the argument of price merely is a more convenient and rational excuse for not buying. It also shields the ego needs from exposure.

Most salesmen appeal to a money-gain or money-saving motive. Sometimes it is a rational motive, for example, in selling resale merchandise to retail stores. But examine it closely in the context of your sales situation. If you sell to purchasing agents of manufacturing companies, who realizes the benefits of a few dollars saved —the purchasing agent or the company? The company, of course. The most that the purchasing agent can expect is recognition (emotional factor) for contributing to the profits of the company. Therefore, the benefit to the buyer is recognition, not money; and the salesman should appeal to this motive.

In those situations in which the salesman sells directly to the user, money-gain or money-saved becomes a strongly emotional motive. Some buyers save money through habit (security). Others make money because it is an obvious badge of power and dominance.

A search for the underlying *emotional* motives of money has saved many a sales interview destined to failure if permitted to continue on money considerations alone.

Security

This is a need for providing safety from economic and physical danger. Many older people are strongly motivated by this need. Their backgrounds may include the depression of 1929–33 or other financial reversals. In addition, they may have arrived at a comfortable station in life where they have accomplished what they set out to do and now wish to conserve their resources.

New ideas, new products or new methods might be hard to sell to prospects motivated by security needs, unless you can show them that security will be actually bolstered by taking the action you suggest. Some new products depend heavily on security needs, e.g., radio-controlled garage doors, storm windows, fire extinguishers.

Fortunately, this need doesn't exist solely in older prospects. Once a man has provided for the necessities of life for himself and his family, he is motivated to protect what he has. A young man, for example, may become a prime prospect for insurance, savings bonds or stock investments.

Belongingness

As security needs become fairly well satisfied, belongingness motives begin to emerge as strong determinants of behavior. This motive is quite broad, as it extends from the affection of intimate members of his family to acceptance of members of his work and social groups. You can observe this motivation in people who feel sufficiently secure in their lifestyles and work: They often join country clubs, work in fund-raising campaigns and become active in professional societies. Recognition by others is a strong "satisfier."

The sex drive is also part of Belongingness. Thus, a wide range of products is available to satisfy this motive, e.g., cosmetics, clothes, autos, food and entertainment, jewelry, diet-aids, tours, etc. Romance is not limited to the younger set by any means. Mature prospects buy to retain beauty, youth and glamour. (Observe those who buy romance magazines at the newsstands!)

This motivation is one of the stronger motivations to buying action. It is probably never completely satisfied in most people.

Esteem

Gratification of esteem needs creates feelings of self–confidence, worth and strength—of being useful and necessary in the world. Pride and prestige are the more ego-centered forms of this motive.

Much of the production in our industries and businesses is directed toward satisfaction of this motive, e.g., expensive cars, exclusive homes, clothing, furniture, food, cosmetics, health products, etc. This motivation is probably never completely satisfied.

Authorities who have spent much of their lifetime in studying consumer motivation maintain that the need to be proud, to feel important, to acquire status, is the strongest of all motivations. Certainly it is the most universally distributed. Management consultant Tom Lawrence tells us that we should think of everyone as carrying a sign on his chest that pleads, "Help me feel important!"

Think of the violent upheavals we have experienced in our society—people crying out "Give me status." How often we overlook this natural human desire, not only in our society, but also in our work: the receptionist whose name we can't remember; the prospect who has valuable contributions to make to the sale, but we do all the talking; the countless opportunities we have to make a prospect like himself a little more by giving him a sincere compliment.

Work efficiency in our organizations has largely resulted in the abstinence of praise. Self-fulfillment from work is in itself a reward to the independent businessman; but the employee of a company usually only hungers for it.

Self–Actualization

This is also called self-realization: the drive to become everything that a man has the potential to become. At this level, a man does not strive for achievement in order to gain more money, power or prestige; rather, his motivation is based upon the personal satisfaction of achievement. Self-actualization is the motive that compels a mountain–climber who, when asked why he wants to climb Mt. Whitney, answers, "Because it is there." It is the motivation that drives men to become presidents of large corporations. Surely, who would want all those headaches when security, money, social acceptance and esteem are so plentiful at a lower level in the corporation? Executives, community leaders and highly-positioned politicians are almost exclusively motivated by this need.

For our purposes, we must translate these rather broad generalizations into more specific sales needs; but first, several observations:

1. People progress up this pyramid and, consequently, the nature of an individual's needs are constantly but gradually changing. Think of the newborn baby: First, food, warmth and comfort are all-important (Physiological Needs). The child is motivated to cry if he doesn't get them. Then, Security is provided by a mother's arms. Then the child begins to relate to the people in his small world (Belongingness). Later, Esteem, maybe in the form of playing second base on the baseball team, is all-compelling. Still later, he becomes motivated by career plans (Self-Actualization). These are immature motivations to be sure, but look for them in your own family. Look for them in your prospects. Look for them in

an entire civilization (the Roman Empire, for instance). This hierarchy of needs is one of the true common denominators of human behavior.

2. People are motivated by unfulfilled needs. For many salesmen, there is little strength in the physical needs—because they are satisfied in most prospects. For most salesmen (with the exception of salesmen selling insurance, stocks, mutual funds, etc.), the security motivation may not be too important.

3. Prospects are motivated to buy if they sense fulfillment of certain needs. The greatest motivation potential lies in the Belongingness and Esteem levels for most products being sold today.

Think Big—An Expanded List of Buying Motives

The number of buying motives is virtually limitless. Every buying action is motivated; however, the motives are frequently mixed and indistinct. In this section are listed some of the needs that can help bridge the distance between a product on the one hand and the mind of the prospect on the other. The salesman's task is to try to produce identification of need with product through his sales interview.

ACQUISITION

We like things for their own sake. People buy, gamble and bargain to acquire material things, not because they have a use for them, but simply to possess them.

RETENTION

Once an object is purchased, the owner becomes attached to it and wants to retain it. The unrealistic demand for a trade-in price on the old car is an example of the retention need.

AVOIDANCE

People are motivated to avoid failure and criticism. They will hesitate to buy for fear of what a superior will say. If they do buy, the salesman may be accused of misrepresentation.

RECOGNITION

Buyers will purchase from a prestige company because such a purchase commands respect. New items are frequently purchased through this motivation. Bigger and more expensive cars are purchased, not because they are "needed" for their extra horsepower, but because of recognition.

AFFILIATION

Some people are joiners; they seek clubs, friendships and associations. They tend to emulate the members of a social and business group in material possessions.

URGE TO CREATE

Because inventiveness has been removed from many routine jobs, people spend much of their personal time in hobbies as a natural outlet for this motive. Model-building, sewing, gardening, cooking, oil painting, woodworking, etc., are fulfillments of this need. Some men even extend this need into creating new business enterprises.

SUPERIORITY

The need to have power over people and ideas exists in many people. New products and ideas are well-accepted when an appeal is made to this motive. Recognition is, of course, part of this motive.

EXHIBITION

Products that can be attractively displayed are received well by people who are motivated by this need. They enjoy attracting attention. Clothes, musical instruments, books and furniture are just a few products that rely on this motive.

DOMINANCE

This need is apparent in many leaders. They enjoy directing the efforts of others. Knowledge-industry products (books, courses, etc.) are naturals here. The drive to earn a great deal of money is also a strong bid for dominance.

AUTONOMY

This is the need to be independent. Many young people respond to appeals in this area.

REJECTION

This is the need to be discriminating. Private clubs, exclusive restaurants, exclusive dealerships, etc., depend in part on this motive.

PHYSICAL FITNESS

In the quest for health we see many mixed motives. Does a man join a country club for affiliation or to stay fit on the golf course? He may advance the latter as his reason; but the former is usually the real motivation. Does a man join a health club to "keep in shape" or to develop bulging biceps to look manly in a T-shirt (sex-drive)? Despite this confusion, the health drive is strong in people; they want to retain their jobs, look more attractive and prolong life.

ACHIEVEMENT

This is a strong ego need in people with high purchasing power. They strive to do things that are difficult.

COGNIZANCE

The urge in most people to know, to learn, to look and to explore is great. Much of the communications industry is based on this need. The reason that most salesmen get in to see prospects stems from curiosity.

PHYSICAL COMFORT

This has to do with the avoidance of exertion and is often the other extreme of the "play motive." Air conditioners, lounge chairs, washing machines, vacuum cleaners and power steering are satisfiers of this need.

IMITATION

"Keeping up with the Joneses" has encouraged many a family to buy a more expensive car or home than necessary. This is a sub–

motive to the needs for Dominance, Superiority, Recognition and Affiliation.

MONEY-GAIN OR MONEY-SAVING

As already mentioned, money-saving may be an intrinsic motivation (habit) that contributes to Security. Money-gain may be a need for Dominance.

The Mystery Guest in Every Sales Interview

Every time you make a sales interview, imagine a third person (in addition to yourself and the prospect) being present. The rules of the game are simple: He has been instructed to remain silent and, subtly and by devious means, to work against your best interests. However, you can enlist his aid (for he is an influential power in your behalf) if you will address yourself to him and identify him. Under these circumstances, how would you play the game?

A buying motivation is a mystery guest to most salesmen; but remember, he is always present and always available to you to further your success in the game of selling.

In trying to further understand buying motivations, the Pyramid of Needs will probably be most helpful. You may be able to think of some variations or even some new motivations. The point is that you must pinpoint those motivations that, in your experience, are most important. Never ignore the secondary motivations; rather, be aware of their existence.

I have found in my personal experience and in working with thousands of salesmen that, for practical purposes, there are only *four basic laws of human motivation* that are important: Security, Belongingness, Esteem and Self-Actualization. Of course, there are several sub-motives present—recognition, superiority, dominance, cognizance and money-gain—depending on the salesman, the product and the prospect. Of the four prime motivations, Belongingness and Esteem are paramount. So, if at the beginning you wish to simplify this rather complex subject of buying motivation, you can do so by considering these two motivations.

Be Aware of Combinations

Sometimes we are motivated to buy with a single motive, for example, when we drive into a service station for a quart of oil. Frequently, however, our motivations are mixed. For example, Mr. Jones comes home and tells his wife about his cute new secretary. Mrs. Jones listens and the following day goes on a shopping trip and buys a complete new outfit. Her motivations were mixed: Belongingness (sub-motive: sex drive), Esteem (sub-motive: confidence), Security (sub-motive: reassurance of position) and Self-Realization (sub-motive: best possible appearance).

One of the interesting facets of mixed motivations is that the total motivational force is greater than any single motive operating independently. Mixed motivations also give the sales person a wider field in which to sell.

Real Reasons Seldom Put into Words

No prospect is going to tell you, "I want to feel more important" or "I want to appear superior to others in my social group." Many of the more powerful needs that motivate buying action are very personal ego needs that a prospect will not verbally admit and, even in his most candid moments, mentally symbolize in their true state. The salesman must interpret or sense these motivations by analysis of what he knows about the prospect, what he observes about him and what the prospect says (more on this later).

Rational and Emotional Needs

As a consequence of the "sheltering" a prospect gives his emotional needs, he frequently needs the salesman to supply him with a rational reason to buy. The rational reason supplies little or no buying motivation, but does supply him with a *justification,* which permits him to keep his real reason hidden from view.

This is a consistent finding in our studies of customers who have purchased a particular item. After–the–sale interviews with people who have bought are generally unsatisfactory because they disclose that customers either don't know why they bought or they try to justify the purchase. The middle-class family member will justify his purchase of a luxury automobile by saying, "It was such a good deal, I couldn't pass it up." You should remember that everyone has two reasons for buying: a good reason and a real reason. The real reason supplies the motive power, the good reason the justification.

There are some important gray areas between rational and emotional motives. One of these gray areas is that of problems. A prospect may be aware of a problem (or the salesman can develop awareness). On the surface, the problem appears to be decidedly rational, but further analysis discloses that it is due to unsatisfied needs and that some of these needs are emotional.

The only reason for stressing emotional or ego-centered motivations is to make you sensitive to their existence and their strength as determinants of buying action. I do not, on the other hand, depreciate the importance of rational motives.

Recycles and Shifts

The Pyramid of Needs outlines a sequence of motivations. As a prospect matures and advances in position, he tends to move up the pyramid. There are many exceptions to this rule. Some people never reach the pinnacle of Self-Actualization and, in falling short, may tend to recycle. Security may assume greater importance. A bum in a flop–house, having scarcely enough food to eat, may make the headlines in your evening paper: "$50,000 Found in Mattress." A man may lose his job and, suddenly, his whole system of motivations can change overnight. When a girl gets married, such things as cosmetics, diet foods and wigs may no longer have the old appeal. And so it goes, each change in our environment exerts its own set of motivations.

The Principle of Projection

Some salesmen never use the great force of motivation, either because they are not aware of it or because they haven't developed the technique of using it. Others, who are aware and make valiant efforts to get motivation to work for them, never really succeed because they make too many mistakes in reading the signs. The problem with this latter group is that they make assumptions about the prospect based on their own experiences in life.

This is the Principle of Projection, which says that we tend to see qualities in another persons that are, in reality, qualities in ourselves. In other words, we all project our own motivations, biases, preferences and hang-ups into our analyses of other people. The swindler will carry on about corruption in society; one person will see another as "slightly looney" because he is not emotionally stable himself, etc.

The Principle of Projection can distort your assessment of prospects unless you know where you stand—what motivates you. Once you determine your motivations, you can make allowances for them in your analyses of prospects. Therefore, I urge you to take the Motivation Self-Analysis Quiz that follows.

Motivation Self Analysis

Here are ten sets of five statements each. Within each set, decide how you feel about each statement in relation to the others.

You are allowed five points for each set, which you can distribute among the five statements depending on the degree to which you agree with the statements. For example, if you strongly agree with a statement, you can score as high as five points and nothing for the remaining statements. However, in most sets, you will probably distribute the five points among several statements. Do not exceed the limit of five points for each set. Write your points in the appropriate columns for easy scoring at the conclusion of the analysis.

Statements

A	B	C	D	E

1.

A. I wish I had more pep and energy.

B. I don't like to move around from place to place.

C. The greatest things in my life

are the love of my family and the respect of my friends.

D. I enjoy being the "life of the party."

E. In games, I care a great deal whether I win or lose.

2.

A	B	C	D	E

A. If I didn't have to eat or "pay the rent," I probably wouldn't work as hard.

B. I want to stay in one location and build for the future.

C. I like to join country clubs, luncheon clubs, etc.

D. I probably spend more for my car, home and suits than my income warrants.

E. I enjoy doing a job well, whether or not there is a reward.

3.

A	B	C	D	E

A. The worst thing that could happen to me is to go hungry.

B. I like firm and strict supervision.

C. I have many friends.

D. Among my friends are some of the more influential members of the community.

E. I tend to work fast so that I can move on to other opportunities.

4.

A	B	C	D	E

A. I see a doctor regularly and watch my physical condition.

B. I wish I had a better retirement plan.

C. I do not like being alone.

D. If I can't get recognition for a job well done, I'm not much interested in doing it.
E. I openly discuss differences of opinion.

5.

A	B	C	D	E

A. I am concerned when I get less than 8 hours sleep a night.
B. I work for accuracy rather than speed.
C. I sometimes do what is pleasing to my family and friends even when I want to do something else.
D. I am talkative even around strangers.
E. I get great personal satisfaction from a job well done.

6.

A	B	C	D	E

A. I wish that I had more time to exercise and keep in top physical condition.
B. I always prepare for a "rainy day."
C. My wife, family or friends have greatly influenced my life.
D. I would enjoy being referred to as an "Ace Salesman."
E. My goals are pretty well firmed up for the years ahead.

7.

A	B	C	D	E

A. My work is so hectic that I can't eat or sleep as I should.
B. I think things through very carefully.
C. I find it difficult to say "no" to

a polite and friendly salesman.

D. I feel uncomfortable in an inexpensive suit.

E. I am constantly trying to improve my knowledge and skills.

8.

A	B	C	D	E

A. I feel happiest when I am at home.

B. I like strong leadership.

C. I try to always understand the feelings of others.

D. I like to regard myself as a very effective person.

E. Moving up in an organization is the important thing—the rewards will follow.

9.

A	B	C	D	E

A. Most trouble in the world could be overcome if people had enough to eat and adequate housing.

B. I get a good feeling by having a sizable savings account.

C. I sometimes color the truth to avoid hard feelings.

D. I'd like to have my associates think of me as an effective person.

E. I sometimes do what I think is best even if others disagree.

10.

A	B	C	D	E

A. If people have inadequate food, housing and clothing, it's all right for them to resort to violence.

B. I usually side with the majority opinion.
C. I would rather work with someone than to work alone.
D. I enjoy winning especially when the victory is recognized by my friends.
E. There are many important things I want to achieve in my lifetime.

Totals ______________________

HOW TO SCORE

Total each column (A, B, C, D and E). Enter scores below.

A. Physical Needs Score______A.

The degree to which you are motivated to satisfy physical needs (food, shelter and clothing).

B. Security Needs Score______B.

The degree to which you are motivated to satisfy security and safety needs.

C. Affection and Affiliation Needs Score______C.

The degree to which you are motivated to satisfy the needs to belong, to gain affection and love.

D. Esteem Needs Score______D.

The degree to which you are motivated to gain respect, prestige and the esteem of others.

E. Self-Actualization Needs Score______E.

The degree to which you are motivated to reach your potential.

Total ______

(must equal 50)

5

How Immediate Sales Perception Provides the "Sensing Action" You Need to Trigger the Yes Response

In his introduction to Basil Rathbone's recording of *Stories of Sherlock Holmes,* Rex Stout says:

> Sherlock Holmes is the embodiment of man's dearest and most stubborn conceit: that he is a reasoning animal . . . Our aspiration to put our reason in control of our instincts and emotions is so deep and intense we constantly pretend we are doing so. We almost never are, but Sherlock Holmes always is.

If you have read even a few of the many Sherlock Holmes stories by Conan Doyle, you will recall that the typical case was attended first by meticulous investigation and accurate observation and, finally, by a few objective questions. There was no "casting a net" and gradually eliminating possibilities; instead, the investigation was a mental and sensory exercise to find the shortest and most potentially rewarding path to a solution.

Selling is not fiction; it is a hard fact of life. It too requires a keen sense of perception to discern the path or strategy that gives direction to the sales interview. With greater certainty, perception will lead to a solution or favorable action for the salesman and prospect alike.

In this chapter we will discuss perception—your ability to develop an immediate, intuitive recognition of the motivations of your prospect so that you can direct your remarks to "where the man lives," so that your product benefits match with the prospect's needs, so that your interview makes extremely good sense to your prospect

To Prosper in a World of Constant Change—Develop Your Perception

I firmly believe that we don't sell the large proportion of prospects we call on because we make the wrong decisions about them. Wrong decisions are, at the bottom, the result of insufficient or inadequately processed information. Sales companies in the distant future may issue portable computers to their salesmen to remind them of necessary "input" and to calculate the strategies open to them. In the meantime we must learn to use our senses more effectively as well as the built-in computors already in our possession—our brains.

Like the rat maze, there is a way through the complex jumble of motivations, needs, wants, desires, emotions and attitudes (some of which the prospect himself is unaware!). The development of a keener sense of perception won't guarantee that you will find it every time; but immediate perception, together with what you now know about the Dynamic Laws, will increase your sales income more dramatically than any single skill you can develop. This entire concept is based on rigidly conducted sales and human behavior research and will add to your sales armamentarium for years to come.

The Three Steps to Extra Confidence in Dynamic Selling

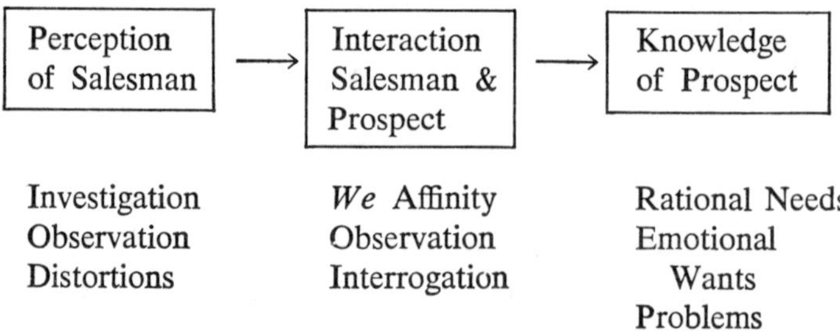

A salesman calls on a prospect or customer. It may be for the first time, it may be a follow-up call, it may be a regular-repeat call. What determines his chance of making a sale?

Assuming worthiness on the part of salesman, product and prospect, the sale depends, in the most abbreviated form, on the *Perception* of the salesman, his *Interaction* with the prospect and his ability to gain accurate *Knowledge* of the prospect. The only possible disagreement might be, "Maybe he doesn't need the product." The "need" is assumed in the statement "worthiness of salesman." This will become clear as we progress.

The simple dependency upon perception, interaction and knowledge contradicts the illusion that has guided salesmen for years, namely, that the right words are responsible for planting ideas in the mind of the prospect. Consequently, salesmen search for a few magic phrases that will raise his buying temperature to new heights. They look for an "angle." They spend hours in writing and memorizing sales presentations, trying for just the right degree of forcefulness, humor and thoroughness. When it's all over, they wonder why such a brilliant show of logic, personality and rhetoric hasn't won over more prospects. Actually, there are no right words without perception, interaction and knowledge.

This chapter will look at the principal ingredients that go into making perception pay dividends to you in the form of an easy, highly professional sales presence—truly, the Dynamic Laws in action.

Investigation is a simple ingredient in selling, and I've always wondered why it is so commonly overlooked. Often, salesmen are satisfied that the prospect's name appears on a route list, that the salesman who occupied the territory previously called on him, that the prospect is in a business that uses the salesman's product, etc.—in short, that he is a "warm body." Valuable clues can be gained by making some inquiries about the prospect (even if you've called on him for years) and doing research in industry publications, yellow pages and newspapers.

Observation is more than just looking. Again, there is a curious lack of interest in visual clues that reflect the prospect's lifetime of living. A man's dress, his office or home surroundings, his speech, mannerisms and gestures are all there for a salesman to see. We should be sensitive to them. We should learn to see, compare, differentiate and draw tentative conclusions.

Distortions of need identifications result from the salesman's inability to perceive, to relate and to make allowances for human errors in sizing up prospects. We will discuss the major distortions so that you can make allowances for them.

Perception in Action: The Famous Benton-McTavish Interview *

You have been briefly introduced to the ingredients of sales perception. Before we go further, I want you to experience the application of these perceptions in a sales interview.

As you read the Benton-McTavish interview, try to identify how each is applied in a typical situation. You will almost automatically identify with Ellis Benton, but notice that McTavish is not unlike many prospects you call on. The lines are numbered so that you can make notes of instances in which each ingredient is illustrated.

The Benton-McTavish Interview

Cast: Ellis Benton—Salesman
Kevin McTavish—Prospect

BENTON: (Slightly Under Breath) Twenty-seven, sixty Beacon Road, check, Seven minutes to nine, let's see (shuffles cards). Prospect is Mr. Kevin McTavish, Vice-President in Sales. Bet he runs a tight ship! (Hmm.) He inquired about our training program through an ad in *Today's Management.* OK. I qualified him over the phone when I called for an appointment. He's in steel fabricating. Employs between 25 and 30 salesmen and covers seven states. Talked with Jim Angle about him—says he's a two-fisted businessman who gets results. Very successful. Worried about losing business to a new competitor in Cleveland. Requires salesmen to wash cars at least once a week and to wear hats on all calls. (Wow!) Portfolio's OK. Well, here we go.

* H. B. Rames, *Synergistic Selling* (Lincoln, Neb., 1971, Panel Book) p. 20. Also available in cassette recording through Executape Systems, Inc., Lincoln, Neb.

Good morning, I'm Ellis Benton. I have an appointment with Mr. McTavish at nine.

RECEPTIONIST: Won't you be seated, Mr. Benton? I'll tell Mr. McTavish you're here.

BENTON: (Slightly Under Breath) Functional reception room. Nothing fancy. Very utilitarian. Trade magazines on table. Address label on magazines is to McTavish at a residential address. Must get them at home so he can read them there.

RECEPTIONIST: Mr. Benton: Mr. McTavish will see you now.

McTAVISH: (Scottish Accent) Come in Mr. Benton, come in.

BENTON: Thank you. Mr. McTavish (Slowly), I have an idea for you, but first, so that we can determine its application to your business, may I ask you a few questions?

McTAVISH: Very well.

BENTON: A survey recently conducted by the Sales Executives Club of New York, and reported in *Business Week,* illustrates that recruiting, training and supervising a salesman is an expensive procedure—some $8,731 per man on the average. Is this figure fairly close to your cost?

McTAVISH: Well, I don't know that it's quite that high. I put my salesmen in the warehouse and plant for about—oh—four months before they go on the road. They're doing useful work while they're learning the business.

BENTON: I see. But if they did *not* work in the warehouse, would you hire extra warehouse people to take up the slack?

McTAVISH: Probably not.

BENTON: Then aren't the salaries and fringe benefits you pay them during training actually *cost* figures?

McTAVISH: Yes, (pause) I presume that's so. And then there are the expenses of supervision. Maybe $8,000 is not too far off. Whatever it is, with all costs going up, it's not going to get better, that's for sure.

BENTON: An important observation. Tell me, what is your average cost per call?

McTAVISH: That is rather confidential. With advertising, expense accounts and company cars it's rather high. We sell tough because we're in a very competitive business. The cost per call is about forty dollars or so but that's very confidential.

BENTON: It will remain confidential, Mr. McTavish. Your cost per call is about average, if that's any consolation. McGraw-Hill's industrial survey reflects a cost of about $50.00 per call—an increase of 200% in the past 12 years. Can you foresee a decline in the next few years?

McTAVISH: None whatsoever. Costs will go up if anything.

BENTON: One more question: Can you tell me the rate of turnover for your salesmen?

McTAVISH: Again Mr. Benton—quite confidential. But it's higher than I like to see it.

BENTON: Your information is safe with me, Mr. McTavish.

McTAVISH: Ten years ago when I had twelve salesmen, I had a very stable group. Then we doubled our sales force. In the past five years I've lost several good men. Why would a man take another job for just $50 more a month?

BENTON: Remember, Mr. McTavish, that $50 looks bigger to salesmen than it does to you. And of course, there may have been other factors which they didn't want to put into words, or simply didn't recognize themselves. Salesmen turnover is another important cost factor in any sales organization—thc figure has been running as high as 30% to 50% per year in some industries.

McTAVISH: Yes, I've seen those figures and, frankly, our rate is not much better.

BENTON: Then, Mr. McTavish, we have three important cost areas: training, cost per call and turnover—costs which are large, and by your forecast are likely to increase in the years ahead. Now, what will be the effect on your net profit if these costs continue to climb?

McTAVISH: (A little irritated) Why naturally our net profit will decline.

BENTON: What solution do you see to the high cost of making a sale?

McTAVISH: (small chuckle) Well, it would be handy to answer that our men must sell more effectively, but that's hard to carry out.

BENTON: A good point: more effective selling may offset a possible net profit decline due to rising costs. I think I have an answer to this problem but first I'd be interested in why you feel it's hard to carry out. Actually what steps can be taken to increase the selling efficiency of salesmen?

McTAVISH: This is a complex question. It encompasses compensation, territory alignment and a host of other considerations.

BENTON: Yes, but aren't most of these considerations fairly standardized operating procedures practiced by most competitive sales companies? Isn't *your* answer to be found in those areas that will give you a competitive edge?

McTAVISH: Of course you're talking about training. Granted, our training could be improved, but four month's training in the warehouse, adequate supervision and quarterly sales meetings. . . .

BENTON: Nothing wrong with these training methods except *will they be adequate to cope with ever-increasing competitive pressures?* Is the record of their *past* effectiveness such that you can depend on them *to offset a net profit decline?*

McTAVISH: Hmm. Mr. Benton, I think you've hit on something. I haven't taken a look at training for a long time. But I like what we're doing. Take our sales meetings—the men go away from these meetings full of enthusiasm and determination.

BENTON: Again, nothing wrong with sales meetings—*if* we don't expect too much from them. For introducing a new product or program—they're great. Men come away from a meeting with enthusiasm—why not? They've had the enjoyment of associating with other salesmen, of rubbing elbows with management. But how much do they take away that's usable information and skill? Recent studies show that (on the average) we forget 42% of something learned in 20 minutes, 66% in a day and 75% in 6 days.

McTAVISH: I hadn't thought of it that way—and sales meetings are certainly expensive.

BENTON: True, and the return on your investment in sales meetings does not grow as any good investment should—it actually declines at a rapid rate.

McTAVISH: Have any answers?

BENTON: If your problem is one of increasing the ability of your salesmen to deliver more profitable sales volume in the face of stiffer competition and rising cost, I do have an answer.

McTAVISH: That seems to be the problem.

I am not going to give you the entire Benton-McTavish interview —for a purpose. What we have covered in the interview thus far is the *difference* between the usual automated product presentation and a synergistic selling interview. This is where we will focus our attention. Incidentally, Benton did go on to present his product and close the sale (a sale which would not have been made because McTavish could not have seen a "match" between his needs and Benton's product until Benton established the problem).

Many sales interviews that uncover needs, wants and problems are shorter than this one. I used an unusually resistant prospect (and consequently a longer interview), so that you'd experience the multiple application of these Dynamic Laws. This entire sequence can be reduced to *one law*—the most important Dynamic Law of them all. Remember this, practice it and you'll develop professional status and income faster than any one thing you can do.

Don't Try To Sell Unless You Have The Same Goal As The Prospect!

Focus on Investigation

This is one of the simpler steps in selling. If it's a "first–time" call, you can't afford to ignore its importance. If you do not investigate the prospect, be prepared for some surprises—surprises that may result in damaging indecision and indirection of your strategy. If you call on the same prospects routinely, you should know quite a bit about them. Do you regard each as different from the others and make notes of their special needs and wants?

A simple question, "Do you know Mr. Blank?" can supply considerable information when directed to neighbors, competitors, service people, customers, employees, etc. Other sources of information include the Yellow Pages, directories, newspapers, Chamber of Commerce reports, etc.

Another method you might consider: Develop a Prospect Fact Sheet. I learned this from a District Manager of the Pet Milk Corporation in North Carolina. He has five loose-leaf notebooks full of valuable information about all his customers! This idea has the added value that you can ask some of the questions of the prospect himself. The fact sheet includes: the prospect's full name and nickname; preferred calling days and hours; job title; receptionist's name; personal likes and dislikes; wife's name; children's names and birthdays; children's accomplishments; home address; church; political party; sports (spectator or active); college; professional clubs; civic activities; and job aspirations. There is sufficient room on each sheet to accommodate a record of calls and the reactions of the prospect.

The nature of your selling dictates the investigative method that will prove most useful to you. But even the most direct, non-personal type of selling (door-to-door) affords an opportunity for you to do some investigation of your prospect and thus to give yourself some direction as to what his "hot button" might be.

Wall Street Journal once quoted Harry T. Ice, Indianapolis lawyer and close friend of Ed Gree, top man at Westinghouse Air Brake: "Before Ed would make a call, he'd find out all he could about the prospect. He never believed in a hit–or–miss approach."

Investigation can be a part of prospecting and qualifying. Here you can save time by being more thorough in your investigation. Be sure you are calling on a prospect whose needs you can correlate with your product. Many sales calls are wasted simply because the would-be prospect isn't really a prospect at all.

The pieces of information you gain from investigation should be thought of only as clues. They must not be considered as firm or final appraisals or judgments. The facts are usually only opinions and open to considerable error. For example, the information Ellis Benton obtained from Jim Angle (lines 9–13) was verified in substance with McTavish (lines 96–132).

Focus on Observation

A woman, who had five days previously given birth to a child, was draped and prepared for a pelvic examination. The doctor, on entering the hospital room, noticed a University of Colorado alumni magazine on her night stand. Doctors are inclined to make small talk while examining their patients, so he observed during the examination: "I see you are from the University of Colorado," to which she replied, "That's amazing, doctor; you can tell *that* too?"

This is scarcely the accuracy of observation I'd expect from you!

The doctor perceived the woman to be a college graduate, due to a sight sensation (seeing the alumni magazine). Much of what we see, interpret or give "meaning to"—we perceive. It follows this sequence:

Sensation + Our Frame of Reference = Perception

We sense heat; but we perceive fire. The interpretation of the sensation is made by our experiences, education and customs—in short, by our Frame of Reference.

Ellis Benton saw a functional receptional room—nothing fancy. He saw trade magazines and determined that McTavish apparently received them at home. His Frame of Reference interpreted these sight sensations into perceptions, which influenced his sales interview. He perceived McTavish as a conservative man who made each dollar work hard; furthermore, he perceived that McTavish was interested in sales improvement and new ideas, and that he was competitive. These perceptions strengthened his investigation—what Jim Angle told him about McTavish.

These perceptions were the basis of Ellis Benton's approach. These also figured prominently in his questions (lines 31–35, 57–61, 101–104 and 110–111). Mr. McTavish's conservative-dollar Frame of Reference was repeatedly alluded to throughout the interview.

Our observations may have important meanings. Look for these meanings. Develop high perception. What can you perceive from the following clues?

Office Building: One newly decorated or one in need of paint? One with marble floors or one that is dilapidated? A new one or an old one? One out in the country or one in the metropolitan area? A single unit or one of multiple occupancy? One too large or one too small?

Furnishings: All chrome and leather or all Salvation Army rejects? Mod or turn-of-the-century style? Hard-utilitarian or plenty-plushy? Colorful-clean or drab-dirty?

Employees: Happy-cheerful or dejected-dreary? Busy-productive or loafing-clock watchers? Well-dressed or sloppy-don't care? Well-trained or "I'm-leaving-Friday-anyway"?

Prospect's Office: Desk tidy or chaotic? Clean or dirty? Pictures-on-the-wall or plain walls? Certificates-on-the-wall or dirty-marks-on-the-wall? Conference-chairs or no-chairs-at-all? Rug-on-the-floor or no-rug-at-all?

Prospect's Person: Good-business-suit or overalls? Well-groomed or a-real-slouch? Mod-hair and clothing or 1920's-style? Shoes-shined or shoes-scuffed?

How do you perceive these visual clues? It depends on your Frame of Reference. As some salesmen go through the preceding lists they erroneously infer that the man in an old, dilapidated building with an office furnished with Salvation Army rejects, employing dejected clerks and doing business in a dirty office in overalls may not be as good a prospect as a man with better surroundings. This may be so; but it may not. Your inference depends on your experience—your Frame of Reference. But that isn't the lesson to be learned here. These are only *clues*—suggestions—to what his buying motivation might be. It is not your place to judge, but instead to find clues—to perceive by observation. These clues may be supported by clues you have uncovered in your investigation. If so, the clue may be more than an opinion. It may be a fact. It can offer you valuable direction in your interview and may be confirmed by subtle questions and responses from the prospect. Usually, no one, isolated piece of information means very much unless confirmed by other investigation, by observation or by questions.

Use Your Eyes + Use Your Head
= What motivational clues are present?

Focus on Distortions

Now let's talk about the "tricks" that our Frames of Reference can play on us to cause our analyses of our prospects to be distorted.

LEVELING

This is a psychological term used to describe the tendency of people to make either favorable or unfavorable judgments. Part of this distortion is due to our disposition to forget the defects of a person in arriving at a favorable opinion, or conversely, to overlook positive characteristics in giving him an unfavorable rating. You've known such extremes, haven't you: To one person, everyone is a wonderful guy, and another person looks only for character defects? Fortunately, most of us are somewhere in-between. But a perceiver's ability to level is a rather stable part of his personality and has considerable influence on his judgment of others.

I ask not that you change from what you are, but instead that you be conscious of this source of distortion. If you usually look at people as being fine, upright and true, that's great, and a wonderful way to live; but acknowledge this personal tendency and look again and closer to discover some of the less desirable attributes in people. On the other hand, if you're inclined to be overly critical of others, train yourself to look for their good characteristics. Incidentally, you'll be interested in knowing that the high leveler has been found to be both more considerate and more observant of others.

PROJECTION

This principle states that we are inclined to see qualities in others that are, in reality, qualities in ourselves. Thus, the salesman who has never learned to handle price objections well will claim that "all prospects are price buyers," primarily because he leaves the door open (projects) for a price objection. The exaggerating salesman is quick to identify the same characteristics in his prospect. The security-motivated salesman concludes that his prospects have the same motivation as he does and, consequently, gives a sales presentation slanted toward security, although this motivation may not be present in the majority of his prospects.

This underscores the importance of "knowing yourself" so that you can avoid projecting your qualities into your analysis of a prospect. Remember, we're all different.

STEREOTYPING

All blacks have a natural sense of rhythm—All doctors are wealthy—All bankers are conservative—And so it goes. We fall victim to the very human desire to classify—to organize the mass of information that we are subject to throughout our lives.

Each person's Frame of Reference has the inputs of personal experience, of what we've been told, of what our social class holds to be true; and these all contribute to Stereotyping. Again, I'm not asking that you change your basic beliefs—only to be aware of their effects on the way in which you perceive people.

SNAP JUDGMENT

Once we have one or more confirming bits of information, most of us are likely to form a final judgment. Snap judgments are surprisingly rigid because, once a judgment is made, we are likely to see and hear only those things that tend to support that judgment.

Throughout this chapter, I have cautioned you to regard personality-revealing bits of information as only clues or suggestions. Avoid forming a "pat" judgment; instead, let it be a suspicion—one that you will try to confirm with later information.

SET

This is our readiness to make a particular response to a situation. It is best exemplified by thinking of a sprinter, dug in at the starting line, crouched forward, tense and waiting for the starter's gun. He "tunes in" only the starter's gun; in fact, he doesn't even hear (perceive) the roar of the crowd. This is "set"—more accurately, it is a motor set. Another kind of set is mental set, as, for example, when you ask a friend to pronounce po-lop-o-nies, you'll probably hear something that sounds like a Greek God (instead of polo ponies) because his mental set was pre-determined by the way you syllabicated the words.

Perceptual Set is a readiness to register and to perceive certain words and actions. It will play tricks on you if you're not thinking. I once called on a doctor in company with a salesman. Customarily, the prospect will ask the salesman to be seated. This one did not. The salesman became so frustrated at not being asked to be seated that he couldn't give his sales story! His "set" was to be invited to be seated.

If you have foolishly made a judgment that a prospect is a "price buyer" (either through investigation or observation), this is your mental and perceptual set. Unless you are very adroit in the art of questioning, you may touch all the wrong bases and end up by losing the sale. You will hear and see only those things that tend to support your set. You didn't see the whole picture.

Set works both ways. The prospect has a mental and perceptual set also. (This we will discuss further in Chapter 9.)

SENSITIVITY

Several years ago, a salesman representing one of the larger and more respected firms called on me. I noticed when I shook hands with him that his shirt was very soiled about the neck and cuffs. We sat down and discussed his proposition. I soon forgot his shirt as we explored a particularly difficult problem my company had. He spoke with confidence and poise. Forty-five minutes later he rose to go. He had to catch a plane for home, some 1200 miles away. Again I observed his soiled shirt with as much surprise as the first time. But it was Friday and he'd been away from home for two weeks. Maybe it was surprising but understandable.

This man had discovered the secret of confidence and poise. He was able to sell, to uncover a prospect's need and to solve a problem —despite a soiled shirt!

The secret of quiet self-confidence and the secret of "heads-up" selling are to be found in Second-Person Sensitivity. The salesman who is uncomfortable in front of the prospect and gives a faltering sales presentation is adversely affected by First-Person Sensitivity.

First-Person Sensitivity is a problem for most salesmen. It is concerned with thoughts of how the prospect regards the salesman. Does he think I'm well-informed? A good salesman? A nice personality? A success at selling? The thoughts are all turned inward. Such a salesman becomes very conscious of the smallest sign that he might have said the wrong word, that he might have offended the prospect, or that the sale is not progressing well. To such a salesman, a soiled shirt could be a major catastrophe!

Second-Person Sensitivity is thinking of the prospect, his needs, his hopes and his aspirations. It's investigation, observation and interrogation all directed *outward* toward the other person (the second person). This is a hard lesson to learn, but it is fundamentally sound not only because it's good sales technique, but also because it adds to a salesman's confidence.

The well-adjusted salesman attempts to master threatening situations by first getting to know what is threatening and then regarding that threat as only momentary. He then directs his efforts toward a more satisfactory course of action. Thus, he is threatened only initially; for he changes direction to minimize the threat. The salesman who is not very well-adjusted either openly attacks the threat or is thrown into a relative panic, which immobilizes his sense of perception.

Perception: A Sensory and Mental Activity

Perception is not only seeing and hearing, it is also "making sense" of what we see and hear. It is relating sensory messages to other experiences, to customs, to impulses, to hearsay, to our own status and image. This we do in our Frame of Reference. It is a very personal thing, and not always in touch with reality. It's more often true than not that sensory impressions are distorted by our Frame of Reference. A salesman should be aware of the pitfalls of leveling, projection, stereotyping, snap judgment, mental and perceptual set and first- and second-person sensitivity, as well as the common sources of error (bias, prejudice and predisposition) so that he can compensate for them and bring his perceptions in line with reality.

6

How to Use the Highest-Paid Few Minutes in Sales to Gain Enormous Wealth

Read this chapter carefully and with an open and inquiring mind; for in it exists the secret of enormous wealth. This concept applies not only to selling (although it will address itself specifically to selling) but to all human (social) endeavors.

At the turn of the century, an Italian economist and sociologist, Vilfredo Pareto, set down a natural law governing the distribution of effort, time, money and other resources in the attainment of results. Known as Pareto's Law, it states that the significant items in a given group normally constitute a relatively small portion of the total items in the group.

Now, this law doesn't mean much to us in its present form, so let's apply it to modern problems. Peter F. Drucker, one of today's foremost business economists, states it in different terms: ". . . A very small number of events at one extreme—the first 10% to 20% at most—account for 90% of the results." * By "events" Mr. Drucker means the resources under our control—time, effort, customers, products, etc. Look at the average sales situation: A relatively small number of customers (10% to 20%) in a territory produce the bulk (70% to 80%) of the sales; a handful of products produce the bulk of the sales revenue; a few salesmen out of a sales force of hundreds produce most of the total volume for the company.

Apply Pareto's Law to your efforts, time allocation, expenditures, etc., and—*if you have an open mind*—you'll be amazed at the

* Peter F. Drucker, *Managing For Results* (New York, N.Y.: Harper and Row, 1964) p. 9.

truthfulness of its revelations. Take the number of miles you travel during a week. Chances are you'll find that only a small proportion of the total miles produce tangible results. If you were to analyze your firm's advertising efforts (direct mail for instance), you would find that only a small percent of it is achieving the bulk of the inquiries and orders. This latter example is nothing new; we've always known it. The problem (yet unsolved) is to identify *beforehand* those customers who are persuaded by advertising. As one advertising manager stated it, "We know 50% of advertising is wasted. The question is: which half?"

You needn't go far to identify the important time and effort expenditure in sales that produces results: It's the *interaction* between salesman and prospect. This doesn't mean that the investigational and observational phases of selling become less important (they contribute to the success of the interaction), but they and every other facet of selling become secondary to the interaction. You can even take this analysis one more step: We have analyzed hundreds of sales presentations and have found that in a 30-minute sales presentation, the sale is made (or lost) within a space of a few minutes—or seconds! It is at the moment when the prospect senses a "match" between his want or need and the product that his decision to buy is made. Everything else is superfluous and much of it is wasted time and effort unless it contributes to the end of need identification.

Take a minute now to turn back to the Benton-McTavish interview in Chapter 5 and identify the precise time at which the sale was made.

Upon re-examining the interview, you probably identified several points at which McTavish started to change direction—times when he acknowledged that he had a need that was unfulfilled (lines 62, 66, 79–80, 86–87). The problem began to narrow and become more precise (lines 98–113). *The sale was made when the problem or need was identified* (lines 128–138). All that remains at this point is to explain the product; and this doesn't call for salesmanship —only recitation.

What I'm asking you to do is to focus your attention on *need identification*. This is the 10% to 20% of time and effort that is responsible for achieving results; this is paydirt! Unless the prospect can see a problem that requires solution, a want that must be satisfied, all the rest of it is just words and wasted effort. It is part of the 80% segment of events that is allocated toward meaningless activity.

In this chapter (and in Chapter 9) we will discuss interaction and the clues your prospect gives you that can lead to identity of need.

Interaction Salesman & Prospect

We Affinity

Observation: Non-Verbal Communication

Interrogation

Listening

WE AFFINITY

This is a mental aura that surrounds people who have similar aspirations, opinions, attitudes and needs. It is a characteristic of friendship but isn't necessarily limited to friendship. Individuals, unknown to each other, can feel a oneness in striving for a common goal. It is a climate that prevails in the successful salesman-prospect relationship.

OBSERVATION: NON–VERBAL COMMUNICATION

Sales observation should not be limited to a "size-up" prior to the sales interview, but must be an integral part of the interview. The prospect will unwittingly communicate signals to you during the course of the interview that will serve to keep your interview pointed in the direction of the sale.

INTERROGATION

This is one of the oldest and yet most generally ignored techniques for discovering how the other person feels about a situation. The questioning technique is so important that a later chapter will be entirely devoted to the several types of questions, when and why to ask them and how to interpret the answers.

LISTENING

Failure to listen is a common deficiency among salesmen. The prospect frequently tells you how he can be sold—vital information that calls for sensory perception (learning) and mental perception (interpreting). When you don't have to remember a standard sales story (which you should not do in Synergistic Selling), your ears and mind are free to receive and react.

Focus on Developing the We Affinity

I have a neighbor who operates an automobile agency. We were discussing salesmanship the other day and he told me of an experience, not an unusual one, but one that illustrates the point I want to make.

"Talk about super salesmen . . . I had one call on me yesterday that was one of the best. He was selling a fire-protection system. Big guy in a $250 suit. A ready smile, a firm handshake, magnetic charm—he had it all! He gave me a sales story that was forceful and dramatic with a lot of showmanship—he even stood up on a chair to illustrate a point! And his close was slick as velvet. I'm not so sure he'd be right for *my* sales force, but . . ."

"Just a minute, Jim," I interrupted, "Did he sell you?"

"No, he didn't; but man was he a salesman!"

Frequently this is the image of a salesman: a glib, fancy dresser who takes command. Surely it's the image to many non-sales people—even to neophyte salesmen. The only people who don't believe it are the real, honest-to-goodness salesmen who may, in fact, be very mild-mannered individuals.

I asked Jim why he didn't buy. This was his answer: "Well, I guess I could use his system, but somehow I got the impression that it was a contest: He against me. It was like a game to see who could win. I could have told him that I was moving my paint shop out of the main building, but I didn't 'cuz I thought I'd be playing into his hands. Anyway, he didn't give me a chance. He did all the talking. Good system, though. Guess I'll talk with Rex Martin over at the lumber company. He installed one last year. Heard about it at the Chamber meeting last week."

Jim revealed several inner needs to me which, if the salesman had *interacted* with him, would have helped to make the sale. But he tried to sell on the sheer force of personality, on strictly First-Person Sensitivity. He didn't allow Jim to participate and, although Jim enjoyed the show, he didn't buy.

It's well to digress for a moment to examine objectives. If I were to ask a thousand salesmen what their objective in selling was, I'd get the answer, "To sell, of course." The fire-protection salesman would also subscribe to this objective. Yet he, and I fear many of us, conducted himself as if selling were only a minor almost inconseqential objective. The fire-protection salesman's true objective was to "sell himself." It's as if he were running for a political office. He wanted people to think highly of *him*. And in this respect, he achieved his objective. It is a strange human deception we practice. Good selling starts with a clear view of the goal.

"Somehow I got the impression that it was a contest," Jim said. This feeling cannot be a part of an interview between two men intent on reaching the same goal. *Synergistic Selling,* you will recall, is a "working together" toward a goal important to each. No longer is it a contest. Each partner to the sales interview contributes his special talents toward goal accomplishment. The goal seldom can be reached without prospect participation.

The *We Affinity* is a feeling of "oneness" in contrast to a feeling of "contest." Togetherness is an important social institution. For instance, members of your social group have similar income levels, tastes and activities. In industry, we have what is known as an informal work group (informal because it's not on an organization chart), which is a group of men or women with similar backgrounds, jobs, attitudes and viewpoints. The important aspect of these relationships is that each member of a group is strongly persuaded and influenced in his behavior by other members of the group. As oneness, togetherness—We Affinity—is one of the natural instincts in people, why not use it to further your sales success? Why not make it one of the Dynamic Laws that motivates your prospects to say "Yes"?

The fire protection salesman did not take the necessary step: to establish a We Affinity. Because he lacked the ability to perceive —to inquire, to uncover, to sense, to recognize the needs, wants and problems of Jim—he didn't sell. The direction of his thrust was inward. He was ego-centered. A simple change in direction, a few inquiries, a keen sense of observation perhaps—in short, better perception—may have disclosed the visceral things, the guts of motivation, the invisible bonds between men that can result in the formation of a sense of We Affinity.

Focus on Observation

Our discussion of observation in the preceding chapter concerned itself with what we perceive *prior* to the interview: the office building, the reception room, the employees, the prospect's office, desk, etc. In this sense, it is *static* observation.

In this section we turn our attention to observation *during* the interview: that is, *operational* observation. It is more difficult to practice. Because the action is fast, instant perception and decisions are necessary. Salesmen generally perform poorly in operational observation. This fact is mentioned, not to discourage you, but to encourage you; for any improvement in this area will bring you generous rewards.

NON-VERBAL OBSERVATION

Every day countless messages are transmitted but not received. It's as if everybody's mailbox becomes hopelessly jammed daily with letters that nobody bothers to open and read. A majority of the letters contain information convertible into money. Others contain vital information that might affect the lives of the recipients. Still others are requests for help from people important to the receiver.

Social scientists tell us that 50% of communication from one person to another is non-verbal! No words are spoken—only gestures, postures, motions, positions. But many of us don't receive these messages. We're oblivious to what is being communicated.

Here is another amazing aspect of non-verbal communication: *Your body doesn't know how to lie!* Because non-verbal expression is not filtered by the conscious mind, it is honest. It is not contradicted by the individual's willful intent to conceal, enlarge, diminish or mislead.

The only limiting factor to your use of this new communication channel is your ability to receive and to rapidly interpret the message. This calls for trained perception: an awareness that non-verbal communication exists, accurate observation during the interview and almost instantaneous interpretation of the signals.

I have an acquaintance who is a deaf-mute. She is completely deaf, and has been since birth. She can observe the same situation as I and come away with twice as much useful information. For example, she can identify nervousness and anxiety in the way people use their hands or their restless pace during a conversation. Guilt is expressed in the eyes and position of the head. Depression is a shrinking body position and a tendency to stay away from a crowd. Aggressiveness is seen in a person's posture.

With the abundant communication being transmitted by the prospect in the form of non-verbal clues that reflect his inner thoughts, why don't salesmen become better observers? Check the following reasons to determine where you may find new opportunities to improve your perception.

Not aware of non-verbal communication.
A little uneasy during the interview.
A little embarrassed.
Thinking of what to say next.
Afraid of what I might see.
It may cause me to change my sales procedure.
Not interested in the prospect.
Looking at sales aids.
Looking out the window.
Looking in my briefcase.
Afraid I might lose my place in presentation.
Not sure of interpretation.
Haven't trained myself to observe.

When I think back on my college days, I am thoroughly convinced that the reason my roommate had more girlfriends pursuing him was because he had developed a strong sense of non-verbal communication! I modestly believe that the same signals were flashed in my direction, but I had to bc hit with a ton of charm right between the eyes to make me aware of an amorous opportunity. Now, of course, it's too late!

But it isn't too late for you to be aware of the opportunities afforded by non-verbal communication in selling. Many good salesmen understand it, have a grasp of the gestures, positions and postures and can relate them to the emotional states of their prospects and be totally unaware of it. If you feel you could benefit by greater awareness, closer observation and keener interpretation, I hope you will try during the next week. You can actually keep a step ahead of your prospects in your dealings with them.

Is Anybody Listening?

Earlier this weekend I was sitting on our patio taking a breather from the arduous task of writing. Over the six-foot fence that divides our yard from that of our neighbors came the voices of two women. It was a spirited discussion about their year's experience with cultivating peonies. After about five minutes, during which time the voices increased in volume as each vied to dominate, it became evident that each was so interested in what she was saying that neither was listening to the other! Now, to vindicate myself with the ladies, it occurred to me that this is similar to many business discussions when one person is trying to persuade another to the value of his course of action. Each person sticks with his arguments to the very end or each finds reason to strengthen his position during the course of the discussion. Neither can see wisdom in the opposing point of view, simply because neither is willing to listen.

Often, listening is merely the pause we grant the other speaker until it's our turn to talk!

Extensive tests have shown that the average businessman has a deplorable listening–efficiency ratio—about 25%. I fear the average salesman is no better. The salesman has some special problems that make listening difficult for him. Selling is a stressful experience. We become overly occupied with ourselves; we turn our thoughts inward; we become concerned with what we have said and with what we will say next. This is the First-Person Sensitivity previously discussed. A change of focus will cure this problem: Practice Second-Person Sensitivity. Think outward; try to determine the prospect's needs and wants. Use questions to help the prospect explore his inner motivations.

A second problem is that we fake attention. This is a natural tendency because we're action people. We're eager to jump back in the discussion with "I know just what you mean, but have you considered . . ." and with that comment we "get back on the track," back to our automated presentation. We don't really listen

—we just fake it. A way to avoid this listening error is to realize that listening is not simply a matter of remaining silent, being passive, letting our own thoughts intrude into what the prospect is saying. Instead, we must work hard to *actively* listen. Good listening, to the surprise of many, requires great mental effort.

A third problem may be that, unconsciously, we don't really want to listen for fear of what we will hear. The prospect can ask a question that is difficult to answer. He might put up a formidable barrier to the sale. This you may find hard to accept unless you're completely honest with yourself. Honest now, can you expect to sell him if a question or an objection stands between you and the sale? Why not get it out on the table where you both can examine it? If the question or objection is untimely, you can always say, "With your permission, I'd like to hold that question and answer it in just a minute." Then be sure to answer it later.

Many of us are only "partial listeners." The prospect starts to talk and we immediately stereotype what he says into a neat package: "A price objection" or "Comparison with competitors," etc. Having arrived at that conclusion, we literally turn off our hearing and start to mentally line up our argument in favor of our proposition.

Another problem common to all listeners, and one that underscores the necessity to *actively* listen, is this: Normal speech is in the range of 125–175 words per minute; however, the ear can handle 300–375 words per minute. As much as 50% of our time is unoccupied and our minds wander. To overcome this problem, two newscasters of yesterday, Floyd Gibbons and Walter Winchell, spoke very rapidly; a team of newscasters, David Brinkley and Chet Huntley (now retired), selected words and ideas designed to create mental imagery. Thus, attention can be retained. Speaking rapidly is probably not very desirable for salesmen, because rapid-fire speech is often associated with pressure. However, speaking of needs and wants that the prospect holds near and dear is to be recommended, for no subject is more interesting to the prospect than himself.

Why Listen? In recent years, members of the medical profession have been listening more and talking less. In a recent article in a medical journal, a statement was made that between 50% and 80% of patients react physically to emotional stress, and that no amount of laboratory tests could find the cause. In these cases, listening is the best therapy; and patients are simply encouraged to talk until the real problem is revealed.

Doctors are now finding that an old but neglected skill is helping them find the key to unlock a therapeutic puzzle. You'll want to use listening skills in selling for basically the same reason doctors use it. Salesmen can find the key that unlocks the sale by listening for it. If they listen, as do the doctors with a "third ear," the prospect will tell them how he can be sold. The key lies in his inner motivation; this we must discover. We have only suspicions up to that time—suspicions gained from observation and investigation—to guide us in the questions we ask. The questions stimulate the prospect to explore his inner motivations. If the salesman listens—*really* listens with a third ear—sooner or later the needs, wants and aspirations of the prospect will be revealed. Once you employ this approach, you'll be amazed at how unguarded people are in revealing these inner thoughts. Until you make a "diagnosis," you cannot employ definitive therapy that will "cure" the prospect's wants. Without a sales objective, it's like using a patent medicine of 15 different ingredients just in the hope that one may work and effect a cure.

Stimulate the prospect to talk; direct his thinking to exploring the need or problem for which your product is indicated; interpret his comments into needs and wants (third-ear listening) and then show him how your product is the answer to the need, the solution to the problem. To do this requires that you *listen* and think.

Three Steps to Double Your Listening-Efficiency Ratio

If you are not now a good listener, it is easy to train yourself. The technique is simple. Here it is in three steps:

1. Summarize the prospect's points.
2. Use key words to remember sentences.
3. Ignore emotional overtones and distractions.

SUMMARIZE THE PROSPECT'S POINTS

This is a most useful technique, not only to improve your listening skills but also to be sure you understand your prospect. Actually, it is a technique in psychology known as Rogers' Rule (named after Carl Rogers, an American psychologist who researched it as a means of avoiding argument and ensuring understanding). More on this in the next chapter.

USE KEY WORDS TO REMEMBER SENTENCES

Much of good listening is memory. The action is fast and, unless you develop some device to assist you in remembering a point, sometimes it will escape forever. Remembering a key word will help you remember a phrase; a key phrase, an entire idea. Also, repeating a key word or phrase reassures the prospect that there is good communication—that you are both on the same wavelength.

IGNORE EMOTIONAL OVERTONES AND DISTRACTIONS

You can never carry the ball and have an opportunity to make a touchdown if you go on the defensive. Trying to justify past actions won't get business. All you can hope for is to regain neutrality. When you work to develop Second-Person Sensitivity, you'll be too busy to let these distractions pull you "off target."

Here is a short excerpt from a sales interview that illustrates the application of all three steps in listening effectiveness.

PROSPECT: We are not unaware of your company and your product. I recall several years ago we looked into it, but we did nothing about it and your company didn't have the courtesy to follow up. We probably felt at that time it was too expensive to retool. Anyway, we found a way around the problem.

SALESMAN: Mr. Blank, from what you've told me, your company did investigate our company and product several years ago. And because of retooling expense, a way was found around the problem. Is that correct?

PROSPECT: Well . . . of course I was not Production Manager at the time—only the assistant. I am just assuming that Mr. Gibson—who was a very frugal man—saw expense as the major barrier. He didn't consult me.

SALESMAN: Then, Mr. Gibson didn't consult you, but supposedly rejected the change-over because of the expense involved?

PROSPECT: Yes, that's correct as I remember it.

SALESMAN: Then, Mr. Blank, may I ask two questions: First, doesn't the problem still exist? Furthermore, do you believe that Mr. Gibson's concern over retooling cost was a valid reason for allowing the problem to perpetuate itself?

Analyze the preceding partial interview to find evidence that the salesman was listening. All three steps in listening are illustrated.

Furthermore, analyze this segment to pinpoint suppositions as to the needs and wants of Mr. Blank. They are revealed in his interaction (or lack of it) with Mr. Gibson.

Finally, notice how this series of questions by the salesman was designed to get Mr. Blank to think and explore. The last two questions are the culmination of the exploration. How Mr. Blank answers them will determine the future direction of the interview.

The late J. C. Penney, writing in Dartnell's excellent booklet "What Every Executive Should Know" * said of listening:

> Its rewards are great, because only then do we really learn something about the other person—his feelings, his ambitions, his hopes, his aspirations, what kind of person he really is, what his gripes are, what his needs are. . . . All this makes for freer and calmer exchange of ideas, opinions and information. As a result, people's minds become receptive instead of hostile. Progress and improvement follow as 'closed-mind-itis' disappears.

The Interaction between prospect and salesman is the smooth execution of those few techniques that make the sale. It's like scoring on the football field—those last few, well-executed plays that put the ball over the end stripe. The team that marches 80 yards but fails in the last 10 yards doesn't win many ball games. This is not to say that marching 80 yards is not important or that calling on the right prospect, preparing for the call, doing investigation and observation are not important. They are. It is to emphasize the fact that a few events out of the many are significant in making touchdowns and in making sales. Finding the need, want, problem,

* J. C. Penney, "What Every Executive Should Know" (Chicago, Ill.: The Dartnell Co.)

desire—whatever you wish to call it—is crucial in selling. Operational observation, non-verbal communication, interrogation and listening are techniques that are indispensable in uncovering the needs and problems of the prospect.

7

How to Sell More by Doing Less—the Dynamic Way

In the 1920s and '30s, the Western Electric Company conducted a series of studies at their Hawthorne plant just outside Chicago. These studies were originally designed to assess the effects of changes in illumination of the work areas, ventilation, rest periods, work schedules, etc.

A strange thing happened. It had been predicted that if these conditions were improved, production would increase. As expected, increased production did follow improvement; however, when these conditions remained the same or were purposely deteriorated for the sake of the experiment, instead of experiencing a decrease in production, the workers actually produced more.

A detailed study revealed the reason for this unpredicted increase. The researchers had inadvertently introduced a human factor into the experiment: In consulting with the workers, they made them feel important—that they were needed and that they were making a special contribution. This finding is now referred to as the "Hawthorne Effect" in psychological literature, to designate the increased positive behavior of people when allowed to participate in discussions and decisions that affect their lives and work.

The Hawthorne Effect is evident in all human relations, especially when our task is one of persuading people to change and follow a different course of action. The reason it is such an effective device is this: By allowing people to participate, they sense that at least some of their individual inner needs may be satisfied in the final decision, which they helped to formulate.

The final decision is always made by the person being persuaded.

In selling, this fact is, of course, obvious. In an industry or business, the worker also controls the final decision. The boss knows that if the final decision is not acceptable, the worker has the options to quit or to intentionally obstruct the success of the decision. The success of a final decision favorable to *both the persuader and the person being persuaded* is greatest when true participation is encouraged—in short, when an opportunity for need gratification is present.

Here's another strange thing about human behavior. We often hear that man is "a goal-striving animal." We hear it so often that we soon believe that if we'd stop 100 people on the street and ask "What is your goal in life?," each would immediately fire back his answer. Not so. You would discover that they would hesitate and stammer, and finally give a confused and probably misleading answer. People cannot readily articulate their goals. Oh, they have them; but many cannot put them into words at a moment's notice. They *feel* them. They are motivated to take action to fulfill them; but they are not "surface feelings."

Detailed interviews by trained psychologists will reveal inner motives, but this procedure is not always practical in the business world because of the time involved. Nor would it benefit us to know precisely what they were at a precise time, because needs are fluid and constantly changing. Therefore, we have to be content with "educated assumptions" and, in a practical sense, these have been a useful base in our attempts to affect change in human behavior.

By "educated assumptions" we mean those assumptions we make of a person's motives based on how other people react to him (investigation), the influence of his environment on him (observation) and how he reacts to certain stimuli (the stimulus of a question, for example).

It will be useful to us as salesmen to know what we are looking for so that our investigation, observation and interrogation may yield the educated assumptions that will allow us to make the sale.

Rational Needs are important determinants of buying action. However, buying is by no means limited to these more easily recognized needs. Continued emphasis on rational needs handicaps your efforts to increase sales.

Emotional Wants, as we have seen, are the underlying, virtu-

Knowledge of Prospect

Rational Needs

Emotional Wants
Problems

ally unconscious "gut" issues that oftentimes are the true motivators to buying action.

Problems exist as a result of unfilled needs and wants. In the truest sense, a problem is not a problem if we know and have available the means by which it can be solved. Some problems can be fairly accurately specified by the prospect; other times, he is only vaguely aware of them. The salesman helps in specifying the problem, in defining its dimensions as well as motivating the prospect to work through to its solution.

To Sell Easier, Raise Your Sights Above Rational Needs

It is rational and logical to think, "If I don't eat I will die." A man faced with such a dreary future will do almost anything to obtain food. Similarly, if your product is so unique and so necessary that no company other than yours supplies it or a reasonable substitute, the rational reasons to buy will be of prime importance. Although we hold our products in high regard, as we should, such a "necessary" product that temporarily has no competitive equal is rare indeed.

This is not to say that rational requirements are of no importance. To the contrary, they must be present for a sale to be made. But their presence in themselves does not guarantee the sale—they only make it possible. Something more is needed to make the sale.

As salesmen, we are deceived into thinking that people buy for rational reasons. Most sales meetings, at which a new product is introduced or a new promotion is announced, are devoted exclusively to the rational reasons why prospects will be interested. In our sales stories, we advance rational reasons to buy. The prospect, on the other hand, advances rational reasons for *not* buying. Although a prospect may decide *not to buy* for rational reasons, seldom does he decide *to buy* for purely rational reasons. So where does this leave you? If you are restricted to rational reasons (to the exclusion of ego-satisfying reasons), the customary sales situation is heavily weighted against you. You can't expect to sell when "not buying" makes better sense to the prospect.

When the real buying motivations are concealed and never brought to the level of consciousness, the discussion works on what is present, namely, the rational reasons (price, product features, delivery, terms, etc.). Let's face it, your rational reasons aren't really that much better than your competitor's. If you push too hard, you convey the impression that the prospect's logic is faulty; and he reacts with animosity, silence or digresses from the subject. These are symptoms that indicate that the true buying motivation has not been uncovered.

To demonstrate this point, here is a portion of a recorded sales conversation:

SALESMAN: Mr. Blank, let me show you why this product is such a terrific buy that we can hardly keep it in inventory.

BUYER: Oh, like that XXX product you talked me into buying last year? I got the initial inventory and then it was "out-of-stock" for three months.

SALESMAN: No, No. We had quality-control problems on that one. This one is getting the whole load on advertising: TV, radio, magazines—the works.

BUYER: Listen Joe, every salesman this morning has told me that. By now, I expect them to drop Archie Bunker just to run the commercials!

SALESMAN: Yeah, but look at this package. It's passed every market-eye test known. It attracts attention on the shelves.

BUYER: Yeah, yeah.

SALESMAN: And for a real quality item the price is very, very low with a good mark-up.

BUYER: OK. I'll bite. What is it—33⅓?

SALESMAN: Our 100-case order gives you an ad. allowance of an extra 5%.

BUYER: OK. I'll put in a token order. Say, whatever happened to old Charlie? I haven't seen him around in a long time . . .

Rational reasons can be argumentative. The salesman often wastes his time with rational reasons unless they truly give him an advantage. The buyer's need for a new product, advertising support, an attractive package and mark-up may not exist, or it may be already satisfied.

What isn't satisfied are his ego needs These are never satisfied. Determine first your position relative to rational requirements. A simple question will do, "Tell me Mr. Buyer, what do you look for in a good quality Dingywampus?" Don't be overly influenced by his answer because it will invariably be a rational reason. Analyze the importance he attaches to it. Does he emphasize it, expand on it or mention it casually and automatically, without much thought? If some doubt remains, another question is in order. "Mr. Buyer, you mentioned low price. At this particular time, is the importance of low price an overriding consideration—more important than, say, an 'ad.' allowance?" Did he mention low price because this comment is the one expected of him (is it the way we as salesmen have conditioned him to respond?) or does it have some special significance?

Once you conclude that a rational need *is* important, then add that extra dimension that you now have as a salesman. Your competitors probably won't have it, but you *do* because you understand the Dynamic Laws. Look for the inner wants that make the purchaser an individual, that make him unique. Show him that not only are his rational requirements satisfied with your product, but also let him sense that his emotional wants will also be fulfilled.

Contrary to traditional belief, rational needs usually are not strong motivational factors in selling. Here's proof: The average salesman's product probably possesses all the rational requirements he could ask for, his sales presentation is built around logical reasoning and yet he sells no more than one or two prospects out of ten!

Think of our efforts to motivate large masses of people to change their behavior. For example, consider the report from the Surgeon

General of the United States on smoking as a contributing cause of cancer, heart disease and emphysema. Conclusive laboratory proof—all perfectly logical and rational. What happened? Cigarette consumption fell off. A few months later it regained its previous level and has been climbing ever since. Most recently there has been a change in the American Cancer Society's TV commercials. Have you noticed? They have changed the appeal from the hard sell of logical, rational reasons to stop smoking, to an emotional theme. Now the commercials tell us of the young, smoking father and his cute son of four years and suggests that he may not be around to take him fishing, camping and to ball games.

The strength of emotional motivation is emphasized again by Ernest Dichter. In his *Handbook of Consumer Motivations,** he says, "People have started wars for independence, and are still starting them, for the right to have their own flag, their own language, their own symbols, which are all *irrational, emotional factors*." **

If your product has all the features that make it a preferred product on the market, be thankful. Now look for the hidden wants of people that will make you the best salesman on the sales force.

Emphasize Emotional Wants and Sell More in Less Time

Throughout this text I have used synonyms to express the thought behind emotional needs. In this section, I turn to "wants," although the word is not recognized in psychological literature as being synonymous with "needs." Yet it does express the thought better. You may wish to substitute "feeling" for emotion.

The dictionary defines emotion as "an affective state of consciousness . . . distinguished from cognitive and volitional states of consciousness." The common emotions of love, hate, sorrow, etc., are very much in our consciousness; however, the feelings that constitute buying motivation are not surface feelings and are probably not often in the consciousness as we think of it. For example, a man may not be aware that he is motivated to buy an expensive

---

*Ernest Dichter, *Handbook of Consumer Motivation* (New York, N.Y.: McGraw-Hill, 1964), p. 418.

** The italics are the author's.

car by prestige wants. He doesn't say (or even admit to himself), "I want a luxury car because I want people to know it's my car when they see it in the company parking lot." Actually, a person tries to keep his ego needs pretty well-buried because, somehow, society thinks of them as being less than moral. The perceptive salesman only "senses" them. Most prospects do not mention them in so many words. But these ego wants are the strong motivations of buying action. The salesman who develops the perception, the feel for them in his prospects, possesses the most priceless commodity of all in helping his prospects achieve satisfaction of their unspoken wants through his services and product.

In Chapter 5 we studied the Pyramid of Needs, so that now you understand some of the broad categories of psychological needs. Now let's take them to the final step and apply them to selling.

Before doing so, let me remind you of the simple technique that will allow you to "touch" these ego wants. The salesman employs a series of questions that are suggested by his prior investigation and observation of as well as his interaction with the prospect. By listening with a "third ear" and by accurate observation of nonverbal behavior, he identifies an experience or idea that may represent an ego want of the prospect. This has the effect of establishing the "ground rules" that govern the presentation of his product. He then presents his product—the goal being the satisfaction of an ego want through purchase of the product. He suggests satisfaction of an emotional want by virtue of the product, being careful all the while not to directly refer to the emotional want by name.

UNDERSTANDING THE PROSPECT'S POSITION

This is difficult if we continue to think of selling as a contest. Synergistic Selling instructs us: "Don't attempt to sell unless you have the same goal as your prospect." This means you must study the other person's position and you must understand it—as he understands it. You must discover why the buyer holds certain beliefs. Only when you understand his position are you able to deal with it.

THE WANT TO BE RIGHT

This want is strong in all of us. It is of no advantage to prove to the prospect that he is wrong, or that he can be right simply by buying. Help him to feel that he *is* right, that he is a capable person and that your product will help him achieve his goal. This throws considerable doubt on the "Yes-but" technique of handling objections. Similar to this is:

THE WANT TO REGARD ONESELF AS COMPETENT, NECESSARY AND IMPORTANT

This point certainly needs no explanation; however, it is strange how often we violate it. A packaged-food company, early in the market development of easy-do food mixes, marketed a cake mix that required only the addition of milk (and presto—a cake!). The product failed; whereas another mix, which required addition of milk and eggs *plus skill in blending the ingredients,* was an overnight success. Housewives wanted to feel necessary and competent in their work. Simply adding milk didn't satisfy this urge. When they had to use a degree of skill in blending eggs into the mix, their want was fulfilled. They probably used many rational reasons to explain their preference. This is the superficial "rationalization" that deceives salesmen.

A product or product presentation that seems to promise the prospect that success can be attained without his thoughtful guidance, presence and supervision, is often rejected. Teenagers seldom buy a car with an automatic transmission. Shifting gears fulfills their want to be important, powerful and dominant.

Be sure you express a labor-saving advantage as one that relieves the prospect from performing unnecessary functions, thus allowing him to use his time and energies in other, more productive ways.

Use the Power of Intrinsic Motivations

We all operate under two sets of controls. The *intrinsic* set includes the basic, social and ego drives—those that result from our interaction with our environment, education, family, religion, etc. —those that exist in our Frames of Reference.

The *extrinsic* controls are those forced on us by direct order, expectations of others or reactions to stress situations. Thus, we find we can sell a purchasing agent who is extrinsically controlled by the preferences of the production manager. We sell the building superintendent because his president is a good friend of ours; or we sell a prospect by using pressure. These are the "angles" that many salesmen choose to develop. Extrinsic motivations give rise to only temporary alliances. Not bad in "one-time" sales, but they are not to be relied upon in repeat business.

The prospect who bought because of high pressure can cancel and "negative sell" your product to neighbors. The building superintendent may try slipping in a few substitutes for your product and, if he "gets away with it," he will continue to do so. The purchasing agent may aggressively seek better credit terms from your competitor.

Intrinsic motivation that makes solid contact with inner wants is stronger and more permanent. There is a psychological explanation of why this is so. Countless studies have shown that people must participate—become intimately involved—in making decisions that affect their behavior. When we overlook this basic rule, we find that people for a time will perform a behavioral task in the prescribed manner, but gradually their performance will begin to revert to the old way or to a way in which they want to perform. They find excuses to explain why a procedure that was forced on them won't work.

Prospects will change their buying behavior chiefly in response to intrinsic motivation. Some prospects buy a little bit from many salesmen. They rationally argue that they want to "pass the business around—keep everyone happy." Of course, no one really benefits from this, including the prospect himself. The enterprising salesman will recognize this and try to make contact with the inner ego wants of the prospect and, in so doing, to solidify his business relationship and increase his volume.

Pay Particular Attention to People with Negative Feelings

It is not difficult to see how positive incentives such as security, belongingness, prestige and self–actualization serve as activators of buying motivation. But how about negative feelings? For example, how about a person with strong feelings of inferiority? Yes, here the prestige and belongingness wants are even stronger. People frequently over–compensate under such circumstances—relying on material possessions to overcome their feelings of inadequacy. (Ride through a poor neighborhood and count the Cadillacs and

Lincolns parked at the curb!) A person who has been frustrated in reaching those goals in life that are meaningful to him may appear to the salesman to be grouchy and cantankerous. The salesman may conclude, "he's not worth calling on." Such an individual may be a good prospect, however, because he compensates: If a promotion has been denied him at work, he compensates with a luxury car or the best house in the neighborhood, etc. He says, "I'll show them."

Learn to Think of Yourself as a Problem-Solver

Most buying motives are basically a desire to solve a problem or to resolve a conflict.

The role of the salesman as a problem–solver is a little easier to accept for most salesmen than the role as amateur psychologist inquiring into a prospect's motivations. Although the latter role is not difficult, a problem can be less personal and easier to discuss. For example, a real estate salesman may identify prestige as a need in a potential customer. Obviously, the customer doesn't mention it in those few words, nor does the salesman acknowledge this want identity to the customer. The salesman-prospect conversation can be less strained, if the prospect proposes a problem by saying: "For the last few years, we have been trying to buy a home somewhere on Tweeddilly Boulevard. But so help me, all the homes over there are terribly over-priced." He expresses his need as a problem. He in fact challenges the salesman to help him solve it.

If a salesman is to participate with a customer in solving a problem, he must know the discipline of problem solving. This is illustrated in Diagram 7-1.

Objective: This is a broad description of purpose, of direction, of mission. It has "reach" in it—something over and above the present performance or level.

Facts: Any facts that pertain to reaching the objective are pertinent here. Inquiry is often necessary.

Problem: A problem is any deviation from standard.

Cause: The set of circumstances that precipitated the problem.

Options: The various solutions that might solve the problem.

Criteria: The standards by which the solutions are judged or tested to find the most ideal solution.

DIAGRAM 7.1

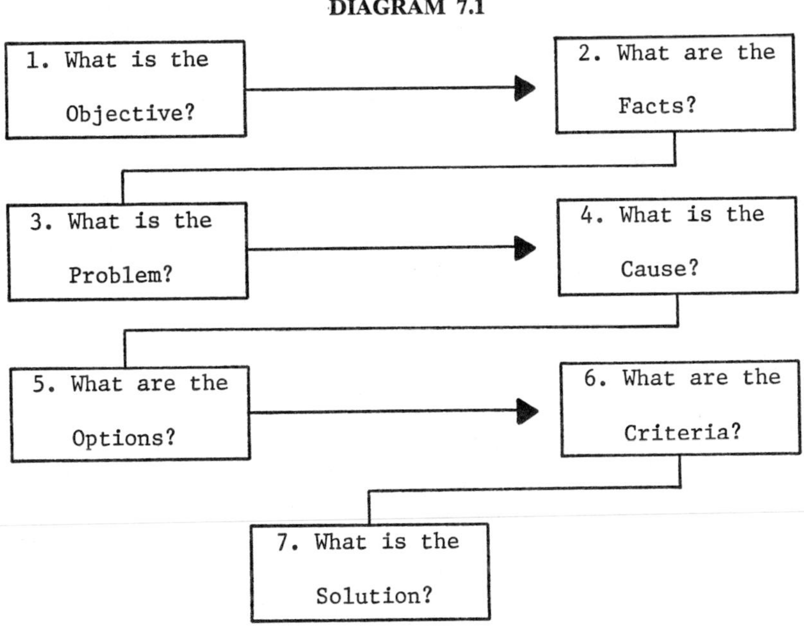

A PROBLEM-SOLVING MATRIX

Solution: The one course of action that has the best chance of solving the problem.

Think back on the real-estate prospect. What are his objectives, facts and problem?

You probably answered that his objective was to find a home in a prestigious neighborhood; the facts were that he only has X dollars in the bank (not enough to buy a home on Tweeddilly Boulevard); and the problem was one of gaining prestige. As the salesman, you might ask discrete questions to ascertain more facts and possibly get some idea as to the cause of the problem.

Such an analysis makes this an entirely new ball game. Do you see the opportunities that exist for an enterprising real estate salesman?

For example, the salesman, knowing that prestige is the objective, might show him a home on Rockingham Road (an equally prestigious neighborhood but the homes are more modestly priced). He might solve the problem by selling him an interest in a new shopping center (thus his nest egg would grow and he'd be associated with other men of means—"owning a piece of the Rock," a powerful motive in some people). Sometimes other alternatives (or options) occur to you that serve to satisfy the need for prestige. Once all available options have been presented, the prospect will weigh them or test them against various criteria. This is essentially a screening process. The criteria the real estate prospect might consider would be cost, time, influence on the people he wants to impress, etc. In this way, he arrives at the best solution for him. Obviously, the more facts the salesman has (especially if he knows the criteria), the stronger position he is in to make a recommendation that is favorable to both the prospect and himself.

The problem-solving approach is a distinct customer-oriented sales appeal because it calls for active prospect participation toward solving *his* problem. It allows the salesman to be very flexible, to change direction frequently during the conversation as more facts become available. Problems are fascinating to most of us—especially when they are *our* problems. The salesman will have no trouble in retaining attention and getting prospect involvement. Truly, the salesman and prospect are intimately participating in arriving at the same goal. The salesman is the catalyst that keeps the action moving. He can influence its direction—point it toward a goal satisfying to both himself and the prospect.

You may ask, "What if the prospect doesn't voluntarily say, 'I have a problem,' but just sits there expecting a product presentation?" Good question. (Of course this is to be expected, because this is the way we as salesmen have conditioned the prospect to react.) This is the way it will be most of the time. Chances are, he hasn't formulated the problem in his own mind or he isn't aware that he has a problem for which our product offers the solution. Also, a prospect may not like to admit to a salesman that he has a problem.

To answer this question, I refer you back to the Benton-McTavish interview (Chapter 4). But before you turn back, let me remind you that, initially, McTavish wasn't aware that he had a problem. At the beginning, he was satisfied with his efforts to train his salesmen. Why? For the best reason of all: He had developed the present system himself. Benton didn't attack it, but calmly called his attention to information that forced McTavish to formulate the problem himself. Once the problem was defined (and not until then), Benton had an excellent chance of success by making his product presentation. Benton's educated assumptions about McTavish (frugal, wants to keep informed, highly competitive) gave him the key to structuring a series of questions toward the goal of getting McTavish to become aware of his problem.

Now you may say, and truthfully, that you do solve problems. I believe it, because most products are designed to solve problems. The difference is how you get into the problem-solving sales interview.

Let's illustrate. Suppose you are an office-furniture salesman. Here's the traditional approach.

> Mr. Brown, how are you? Our company has developed a new modular line. It's all built around this Expando-flex unit, which has gaskets on three sides to receive additional units as need and growth dictate. With these units you can coordinate color schemes or assort in many imaginative color contrasts. Notice the flexibility of this basic design . . .

Here's the problem-solving approach (same product, same salesman).

> Good morning, Mr. Brown. I think I see a way that you can open up the claims-approver office and make it appear less crowded, provide 25% more usable space and anticipate a 10% expansion factor for future growth. May I show you?

Unlike Ellis Benton, the furniture salesman has proposed the problem. Why? Because the problem is more apparent and Mr. Brown is already aware of it.

There are several features that recommend this problem-solving approach. First, it is distinctly "customer-oriented"—it develops attention and interest. The traditional sales presentation is company- and product-oriented and is dishwater dull. Second, it develops less buyer resistance. It says, "I'm here to help you." The traditional approach says, "I'm here to sell you something." Third, it invites participation.

Do you also see opportunities for ego-gratification in the problem-solving approach? Yes, indeed. You can almost hear Brown now talking to the president, "Yes, J. P., and I've built in a 10% expansion factor!"

Here is a step-by-step formula for developing the problem-solving approach. You use the same words, just change the sequence.

1. Consider the problems that your product can solve.
2. If the problem is apparent to the buyer, tell him "I think I can see a way . . ." and list the results he can expect.
3. If the problem is not apparent, what facts can you use to help outline, delineate or define the problem? What questions will you use to cause the prospect to "think-through" to the problem?
4. Once he begins to see the problem, help him to solidify it with such a question: "Very well, the problem seems to be XYZ. Are there other factors (name a few) that we should consider before going on?"

Try this week to look for and touch the ego wants of your prospects. You'll be a little awkward at first; but hang in there. It's magic, and you'll never return to traditional methods. Study and apply the problem-solving technique. It's easy to use and you'll find you can sell more in less time.

Getting the prospect to participate in the sales interview is both the easiest method and the most productive for the salesman. True participation is seldom gained through rational considerations (product features, delivery, color, credit terms, price, etc.) but the intrinsic motivations of people allow a whole gamut of opportunities to the salesman eager to increase his sales power the Dynamic way.

8

How to Capitalize on the Dynamic Law of Asking Questions to Close Sales Faster

Several years ago, a close friend of mine found it necessary to consult a physician. He is a high-powered top executive who constantly lives under mounting business pressures. He was convinced he had ulcers, high-blood pressure, heart trouble and other ailments that combined to rob him of sleep, cause him to be short-tempered with his associates, make him a less effective manager and precipitate countless conflicts at home.

Under the understanding care of his physician, he soon returned to his old, confident self. I saw him at a social gathering several months later and he enthusiastically reported, "I've found a new technique! 'Persuasive probing,' I call it. That bout with the doctor not only gave me a better understanding of myself, but I discovered a new way to get people really motivated. You know, all 'old doc' did was to ask me questions. He didn't write a single prescription, or confine me to the hospital or lecture at me—just asked me questions! He made me find the problem myself. I had the answer in me all the time, but I couldn't define the problem or clarify the issues. His questions forced me to think out the answer. Since that time, I've used this new questioning technique in my business—counseling with my employees, for instance. It's loaded with potential."

My friend hadn't really discovered a new technique. He rediscovered an old technique. Actually, it dates back to Socrates (469–399 B. C.), who believed that his calling was to search for wisdom both for himself and for the Athenian intellectuals. He pursued his calling by using questions that caused his students to examine facts and their implications and, thus, arrive at certain conclusions. Interestingly, the conclusions were the lessons to be taught! Socrates didn't *tell* or lecture his students; but structured his questions so that a particular facet of wisdom was the only logical conclusion to be drawn.

Socrates probably didn't know then why his methods were so effective. We know now. People resist ideas generated by someone else. Outside directives inculcated to bring about change will usually be ineffective. The strategy is to use questions to lead people to the idea. Once *they* formulate the idea, *they* accept it readily because *they* believe *they* thought of it.

Questions serve other purposes as well as getting acceptance of an idea. All of these purposes help the salesman in so many ways that it is a small wonder that questions are not more frequently used in the most personal of all human interactions—selling.

How Questions Can Become Your Most Powerful Ally

Thinking for a purpose is work. You've discovered that already in this book. When you first attempt to apply the Dynamic Laws in front of a prospect, you'll discover that it's very real work. (That's why I suggest you don't wait until you have completed reading the entire book, but apply the lessons in each chapter as we come to them.)

It is more pleasant to mentally drift, to think about goals achieved, victories won—all those mental illusions our minds conjure up to bolster our self–image. Your prospect is likely to feel that way if he isn't playing an important role in your sales presentation. In short, if you are not allowing him to participate and think, he might as well let his mind drift and think his thoughts and not yours.

Questions that challenge him to think about his needs and problems (for which your product is designed) are the most effective instruments to get him involved in your sales interview. As Jesse S. Nirenberg, Ph.D. points out:

> The question is a remarkable conversational instrument. When used skillfully it can point the way to the solution of a problem. It can give an individual insight into his own feelings and motivations or those of another person. It can arouse a mind from its inertia and set it into motion.*

As we review the purposes of questions, try to imagine how you might use questions to serve your objectives in selling. In later chapters we will apply them in actual sales situations.

1. To Test and Influence Readiness. A good question will determine the prospect's willingness to mentally participate in a consideration of your product. At the same time it tends to ensure that if his willingness is marginal, his readiness may be increased with the realization that the ensuing discussion will be meaningful to him in terms of need, satisfaction or problem solving.

Countless times, I have given my sales presentations to prospects who *should* have been interested—but weren't. And, as I look back, I realize that it was my error; for I made no effort to influence their readiness.

You can determine the prospect's state of readiness with a question similar to this:

> Mr. Businessman, I'll need about ten minutes and your permission to ask a few questions. Is that okay, or shall I come back?

You can gauge his state of readiness and influence it favorably with this question:

> Mr. Sales Manager, I think I see a way that your sales volume may be increased by as much as 30%, at a cost of only 0.5% of total volume. May I show you?

Readiness is an emotional state. Questions involve the prospect in ways that are meaningful to him. When you ask a question related to your call objective, you not only favorably influence the prospect's state of readiness, but also you gain invaluable feedback (both verbal and non-verbal).

I'll tell you why questions early in the interview are so crucial

---

* Jesse S. Nirenberg, *Getting Through to People* (Prentice-Hall, Inc., 1968).

to you. We have found in selling, as well as in education and supervision of employees, that once a prospect, student or employee indicates a desire to participate in a subject interesting to him—one that suggests need–fulfillment or that a problem will be solved—he will continue to the natural conclusion with only occasional guidance and encouragement.

2. To Get Attention and Arouse Interest. As a salesman you are an interruptor of your prospect's day. You ask him to temporarily set aside activities that have previously occupied his mind and body—activities that seem (to him at least) more important, more pleasurable and more rewarding. This constitutes a tough assignment for any salesman, especially those that insist on talking about the weather, the state of the prospect's health or "I have a new product you may be interested in."

If, on the other hand, you make an early bid for his attention, his thinking and his participation—with a question—you have jumped the first hurdle of inattentiveness in making the sale.

Here are a few attention-stimulators:

> Tell me, Mr. Retailer, what must a single square foot of counter space earn for you in a month to be profitable?
>
> Mr. Office Equipment Purchaser, if I could show you how, through a new purchase arrangement, you could free-up close to $10,000 in capital and provide trouble-free maintenance on all your typewriters for five years, would you be interested?

Prospect interest is an important conditioning factor in selling, i.e., when the prospect responds in a positive way to a problem or consideration, you have "conditioned" him to positive responses throughout your interviews as you continue to build on need fulfillment or problem solution. A question that challenges, that appeals to a prospect's experience and background when given early in the interview, is a positive form of motivation.

Questions at this point determine the direction of the sale. They cause the prospect to think along the lines that you feel are more expedient to conclude the sale. You, in effect, have turned the prospect in the direction of the conclusion that you desire.

3. To Ascertain Motives. Again, we come back to the basis of Synergistic Selling: All buying behavior is motivated by the prospect's conscious or unconscious desire to satisfy needs. Every sale, in the final analysis, takes place between individuals. If it's a one-to-one relationship or if you are selling a buying committe, individuals are dealing with individuals. Your problem as the salesman is to determine what needs they represent—either singly or as a group.

The problem is simply solved with questions. The prospect isn't often going to tell you his personal needs (because many are ego-needs, which he keeps covered); so you must be alert to clues that reveal his motivation. It is necessary for you to listen carefully and to observe his mannerisms and gestures. Does he repeat phrases? Does he change his position? How does he justify his opinions? Is he an independent thinker or does he follow? What rewards are important to him?

4. To Develop Awareness of a Problem. The sales–incentive salesman, through a series of indirect questions, makes a sales manager aware of the expensive problem of peaks and valleys in sales volume and production. He "sets the stage" for the presentation of incentives to elevate the valleys and normalize sales production.

The doting parents become aware of their awesome responsibility to educate Junior by questions directed to them by the encyclopedia salesman.

The problems of handling an increasing amount of paperwork in a rapidly growing business become the concern of an office manager when gently questioned by an enterprising office–equipment salesman.

A department store executive becomes aware of the mounting cost of keeping his old trucks in repair by the new truck salesman.

"Awareness" is intrinsic—something that happens within. It can't be forced on the prospect from outside. So you do the smart thing. You cause the prospect to come to the realization himself through the gentle stimulation of questions.

Selling is problem-solving, not argument-winning.

5. To Promote Understanding. Understanding is not possible with two persons of different views. If you profess to have the same goals as the prospect, questions can promote understanding because they help clarify meaning. This can be accomplished through questions that call for explanations, comparisons, statements of cause–and–effect relationships and corrections of errors.

Explanation: Would you explain what you mean by the markup not being sufficient to cover overhead?

Comparisons: In what respects does our offer differ from the one you had in mind?

Statements of cause-and-effect relationships: (These are especially good questions for a salesman because they make the prospect think more critically.) Why do you believe the XYZ Company has announced a general price reduction? Or what would be the result of the continuance of this practice?

Correction of errors: (The salesman can correct—partially or wholly—erroneous statements or conclusions, without damaging the prospect's ego.) What experience have you had with our firm that would tend to contradict that statement?

6. To Develop New Insights. If the salesman simply guides the discussion with questions, it is surprising how prospects can develop new ideas and concepts without being told. Remember, the ideas they "discover" are infinitely more important to them.

Question: In addition to greater safety, what other advantages do you see in the new nylon retroactive gears? A: Why they won't need lubricating!

7. To Help Strengthen Your Position.

Question: What features of the overhead cam do you consider most important?

Question: What features of this program will help you achieve your goal of increased sales?

8. To Stimulate Critical Thinking.

Question: In what ways can this procedure be simplified?

Question: What savings can be made as a result of this new device?

Question. The XYZ Company thinks it is necessary to put 50 pounds of tension on their reinforcing wires. What do you think is the reason for their decision?

9. To Test for Achievement of Call Objective. (More information on call objectives in Chapter 10.) A retail tire salesman has determined the type of driving the prospect does, the make of car and a general idea of his price range. He follows with a brief, informative presentation of the composition of the several kinds of tires he offers. Then the test question: "With your requirements in mind, which tire, the Champion (which is built for high speed performance) or the Urbanite (which is built for the stop–and–go traffic of the city) is best suited for your needs at this time?" The prospect will invariably make the correct choice and, having made the choice *himself,* will probably buy. The question is a better technique than the usual procedure of making a forceful recommendation for one or the other tire. The choice is now between one tire or the other, not "Yes, I'll buy" or "No, I want to look around."

10. To Give Direction to the Sale. There is probably no single explanation more important to account for poor sales performance than the fact that much of what is said by a salesman is of little interest to the prospect. In the traditional sales presentation, the salesman, by necessity, talks of matters that *he* feels are important. Failing to address the individualized needs and problems of the prospect, the salesman loses prospect interest, participation and active listening.

As needs and problems vary in identity and intensity with each prospect (no two prospects are alike), can the salesman be held responsible for this indirection? Yes, for only *he* can uncover these all–important determinants of buying action. He does so through the use of questions.

Mayer and Greenberg * employ a useful analogy to explain empathy, which is equally applicable to the use of questions to "zero-in" on the targets of prospect need and problem:

---

* David Mayer and Herbert M. Greenberg, *What Makes A Good Salesman* (Harvard Business Review, July–August, 1964, pp. 119–120) and quoted in: Joseph W. Thompson, *Selling: A Behavioral Science Approach* (New York, N.Y.: McGraw-Hill Book Company, 1966), p. 203.

> A parallel might be drawn in this connection between the old antiaircraft weapons and the new heat-attracted missiles. With the old type of ballistic weapon, the gunner would take aim at an airplane, correcting as best he could for windage and driftage, and then fire. If the shell missed by just a few inches because of a slight error in calculation or because the plane took evasive action, the miss might just as well have been by hundreds of yards for all the good it did. . . . On the other hand, the new missiles, if they are anywhere near the target, become attracted to the heat of the target's engine and regardless of its evasive action, they will finally home in and hit their mark.

Reciting product features is similar to the old anti-aircraft batteries: You hope one might be of interest to the prospect. Using questions to pinpoint needs and problems is similar to using the newer missiles to "zero-in" on the one or more needs most important to the prospect.

How to Use the Right Question at the Right Time

If you want to use questions to discover what the prospect is thinking and what he is striving for, you must know something about how questions are structured to serve special purposes.

Permissive Question

The permissive question, customarily used at the beginning of the interview, simply asks permission to ask questions. (See Benton-McTavish interview, lines 27–29.) Its use may seem overly "nice" to you; yet it is an important "stage–setting" vehicle for two reasons. First, it is a refreshing departure from the "I have a new product to show you" or "I wanna talk to you about . . ." and promises a stimulating conversation, which captures attention. Second, as the salesman is going to ask questions, it overcomes the prospect's feeling that he is being "pumped" for information. Furthermore, it is honest evidence that you are an empathetic salesman.

Make it one of your "workhorses"—it will serve you well in creating a sense of readiness.

Verifying Question

"Mr. Production Manager, I understand you are planning an expansion of your plant facilities. Is that correct?"

This is a verifying question. It results in confirmation or denial of the accuracy of your information. It also introduces the topic for discussion. It is prospect-oriented and invites his participation. You can learn a great deal about the prospect in the way he answers such a question.

Developmental Question

"How do you see this new procedure being used in over-all production in your plant?"

The developmental question is a *how, why,* or *what* question: "*Why* will Mary and Jim need a good reference encyclopedia in the years ahead?" "*What* problems may precipitate a need for additional capital?" Answers to such questions reveal how the prospect reacts to a challenge. They get him thinking precisely along the lines you want him to think!

You probably know that a question that can be answered "Yes" or "No" doesn't really give you much information, nor does it cause the prospect to do much thinking about his position. If you use Yes-No questions, the developmental question is easily substituted by use of one of the helpful pronouns (who, what, why, when, where, or how).

"Can this procedure be used?" (Yes-No)

"How do you see this procedure being used?" (Developmental)

Evaluative Question

"What further information is required before arriving at a decision?"

"What problems do you see in making this operative?"

These questions are similar to a Trial Close (Chapter 10). They test or evaluate the prospect's position relative to your proposal.

They bring out motives that may have remained hidden up to this time.

How to Use Questions to Score

You wouldn't think of using a tack hammer to drive a railroad spike or a coping saw to cut a 4 x 4 timber. Similarly, there are certain rules that govern the use of questions. The following rules are from the programmed textbook, *Synergistic Selling*.*

Question Principle No. 1

The first question should be broad—not specific.

Begin with questions easy to answer—but those pointed in the direction of the sale (Keep "How's business?" etc., to a minimum). The first question should be either a permissive question or a verifying question.

Seldom should you start by mentioning your product. This says "I'm here to sell you something. Now you just sct there and listen." This turns off prospect participation. It is distinctly salesman-oriented.

Instead, start by probing for need or problem (as you do with both the permissive and verifying questions). Make the prospect know you're there to help. This attitude invites prospect participation because you're talking about him and his problems. This is prospect-oriented.

Question Principle No. 2

Don't ask for a commitment of position early in the interview.

Many a sales negotiation is tied in knots when the salesman asks the prospect to commit himself before he has the opportunity to consider the proposition. He says something similar to this: "You have undoubtedly heard of the Blank Land Development Company.

---

* Hank Rames, *Synergistic Selling* (Lincoln, Nebr., Springboard Associates, 1971), pp. 59–64.

How do you feel about owning your own ranch in beautiful Arizona?"

What happens? The prospect either freezes or, being an outspoken individual, takes a position. If he freezes, he won't enter into the discussion. If he takes a position, he does so with insufficient information, and is reluctant to change his position later on.

Question Principle No. 3

Don't ask a question that can be answered Yes or No. "Do you like this new safety shield?" This question should be rephrased: "Under what conditions would you find this new safety shield important?" The latter question permits discussion. If you're asking questions to elicit information, to disclose needs, to get the prospect to think, then avoid questions that can be answered Yes or No.

Question Principle No. 4

Avoid questions that imply criticism.

This is a rather natural tendency, especially when answering objections. "You mean to tell me you didn't send in your warranty card?" is guaranteed to turn off the conversation. "How do you feel this might have happened?" gets to the base of the problem with greater chance of acceptance by the prospect.

Question Principle No. 5

Don't use questions to score a point.

Use questions for their intended purposes—to gain more information or to clarify. Which question is better?

1. "Something you just said seems very important to our discussion; let's see if I understand. You believe that . . . Is that so?"

2. "I'm not sure of what you mean. You surely don't mean to say that . . . Do you?"

Obviously, No. 1 is less offensive. Another good question gimmick to get more information or to clarify is the two-word question, "For instance?" This allows the prospect to move from a generality to a specific and you gain invaluable insight as to how he reacts to situations.

Question Principle No. 6

Use questions to test and give direction.

Some first-person sensitive salesmen intersperse their explanations with these questions: "That's obvious, isn't it?" "See my point?" "Simple isn't it?" The implication is strong that if the prospect answers "No," he is either difficult or stupid.

Practice empathy. Put yourself in the position of the prospect. Isn't "Have I adequately explained this feature?" a better question?

The listening salesman must assume the responsibility of keeping the interview on-track—proceeding toward a goal. Talkers (you included) often get "off-track" and bogged down in trivia. A prospect who starts out by saying that there are three considerations important to him in buying a Dingywampus usually gets so wound up in his explanation that he gets no further than number one. Be a careful listener. Pull the prospect back to the main thread: "I think you have an important observation there. Now I'm interested in knowing: What other considerations do you believe are important?"

How to Link Strategy With Sequence of Questions

Deciding on strategy in Synergistic Selling requires not only some pre-call planning, but also adjustments during the interview to allow you to zero-in on target. The rationale of this procedure is that, despite conscientious pre-call investigation and observation, you collect at best only suspicions of needs and problems. It is necessary in the beginning to follow the path suggested by these suspicions; but accept them as tentative and subject to change as the interview proceeds and you gain further information.

Thus, your position is quite similar to that of a detective who, at the beginning of an investigation, has only bits and pieces of information—any one of which may be either important or immaterial. A suspect may have been absent from his place of business on the day of the crime. This information may not be important, but it's all the detective has to work with, so he pursues it. His interviews disclose that someone saw a man bearing a resemblance to the suspect at the scene of the crime. The strategy of following this path becomes strengthened. A topcoat is found stained with the victim's blood. Investigation discloses that the topcoat was purchased by the suspect. "He knows more than he is telling," reasons the detective. He interrogates him and discovers that on the day in question the suspect and the victim had a violent argument. At this stage, the detective is intent on finding a motive. Once this is established and if the rest of the pieces fit, he probably has a strong case and the suspect may admit his guilt. And so it goes. Bits and pieces of information gained from investigation, observation and interrogation: some that must be discarded, some that fit and, in the end, produce a mosaic of meaning.

You, as a salesman, also come into the interview with only bits and pieces of information; but this establishes a tentative pattern to pursue. The responses to your questions determine what is and what is not important. Two complementary pieces tend to suggest a need or problem. You follow this line of reasoning. It is confirmed or it is rejected. At this stage, you must be content to find the motive. Once this is established, if your product "fits," your prospect will probably agree to buy.

The objective of the detective during the investigative phase of a crime is not to get conviction. Similarly, the salesman's objective during his investigative phase is not to sell. Both investigative activities are directed toward an accumulation of pertinent facts that will disclose a motive—in the case of the salesman, to ascertain both for himself and the prospect the psychological need or the problem.

Let's illustrate this technique by referring again to the Benton-McTavish interview. Benton, in his pre-call planning, started with the known suspicions. Review everything up to the first words spoken by McTavish (lines 1–23). What are the three known suspicions?

Suspicion #1. (Considering the trade magazines and the fact that they were addressed to his home) McTavish has a strong need to know—an informational *need.*

Suspicion #2. (Considering the austere office and Jim Angle's comments) McTavish is very cost conscious—the *need* to save money.

Suspicion #3. (Considering Cleveland competition) McTavish has a *problem:* how to increase sales volume and keep profits stable.

Next, find the questions that Benton asked that made contact with these needs and encouraged McTavish to think through to a definition of the problem. Each question was meaningful to McTavish because it was addressed to the needs that Benton suspected motivated McTavish.

1. Cost of training and supervision of salesmen.
2. Cost per call.
3. Turnover of salesmen.

Each question and its response led easily to problem specification (lines 109–137). McTavish's problem was determined: to increase his sales volume and keep profits stable. Benton's goal was clarified: how to improve sales effectiveness.

You can plot your strategy on a matrix similar to the one that follows. Notice that you start with the suspicions and develop broad and general questions. As you gather more information and as needs are identified, the field narrows until you zero-in on the target —the problem.

Keep this graphic representation in mind as you plot the sequence of questions you will use. Follow the sequence of Permissive Question ⟶ Verifying Question ⟶ Developmental Question ⟶ Evaluative Question. Once you suspect a need, ask further questions, recycle the sequence, try to get a combination of bits and pieces that clarify the needs and point toward a problem. A problem is, after all, one need or several needs that remain unsatisfied.

Once the problem is exposed, a simple question puts you within scoring distance of a sale. Something like this: "Am I right, Mr. Prospect, in assuming that if I can show you a way that (the problem) can be overcome, you'd be interested?" Guided by the prospect's needs, you explain how the problem can be overcome with your product.

Someone once described a detective's job as "collecting string." If he collects enough pieces and he ties them all together, he can make a ball. This is your job, too. Through involving your prospect in dialogue directed toward *his* needs, you make contact with

DIAGRAM 8.1

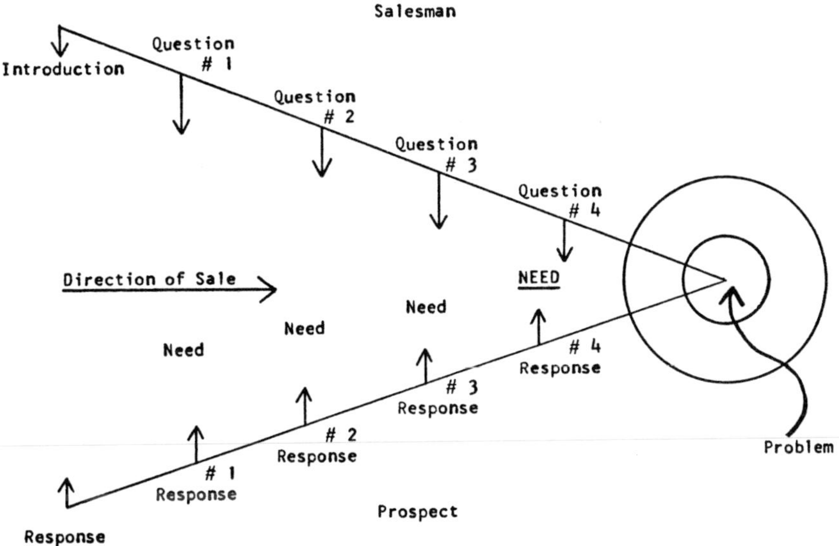

A Matrix of Questions and Responses
To Reveal Needs and Problems

the most responsive part of his being. Now, can you tie them all together and find a problem that your product can help solve? If you can—you'll have a ball, and more rewards from your work.

9

How to Tap Your Magnetic Sales Personality by Using the Simple, Two-Step Dynamic Law

Sooner or later it must happen. We must apply principle to practice; and that is where we are now.

Suddenly, at this moment, you must become more involved in the Dynamic Laws. In the preceding chapters, you were more or less a passive recipient of information. Now you must enter the mainstream and become a part of it.

If you are like most salesmen, you are tapping only a small fraction of your sales potential—your magnetic sales personality. You are literally much better than you think you are and, if you will permit yourself, you can become truly a great salesman.

I do not imply that you are a poor salesman. You don't have to be a poor salesman to get better; but the obvious often eludes us. You can employ an easier manner in your selling. You can be warmer, more open and honest, more responsible and responsive. You can make more sales calls, write more business, be more creative and avoid the "hard work" that often accompanies sales work when reliance is placed on pressure tactics. All of these possibilities are within you. They are part of your potential.

We have talked about buying motivations. You now have a new knowledge of sales perception. You understand the technique of asking questions. We are now going to put it all together. What you will learn in this chapter has been tested and refined in actual sales practice. It will help you achieve your sales potential and encourage your sales growth. It will raise your level of return for your effort and thoughtfulness.

I told you that the Dynamic Laws can be incorporated into your present sales procedure with very little modification of your present procedure. I still maintain that this is true. Of course, you are aware that important changes have taken place in you—in your attitude toward selling. In your present sales procedure, just three changes are necessary:

1. *Insert a new step between the Approach and the Product Presentation,* which we will call "Survey." This usually does not make the sales interview longer; actually, it shortens the Product Presentation.

2. *Shorten the Product Presentation.* Instead of a complete discussion of *all* features of your product, present only those that satisfy the predetermined needs of the prospect or those that contribute to the solution of his problem.

3. *Place less reliance on pressure tactics in the close.* The close is often not necessary when the Dynamic Laws are used correctly. When it is necessary to help the prospect make up his mind, use a low–pressure close.

If you want to begin to be all that you can be, revaluate your present sales techniques in light of what is being presented here. Remember, you have the capacity for considerable growth in sales effectiveness—if you use the full potential of your magnetic sales personality.

> Compared with what we ought to be, we are only half awake. Our fires are damped, our drafts are checked. We are making use of only a small part of our possible mental and physical resources.
>
> —William James

1. The Approach

WHERE YOU ARE

- At this time you know your product thoroughly and its application to the prospect's business or personal life.
- At this time you know as much about the prospect as is reasonably possible through investigation and observation.
- At this time you have made some broad assumptions about him and have a tentative sales strategy.

The approach is a very simple one. It is very short, and it has only one purpose. Imagine a situation. You are in a stadium or in front of your TV watching your favorite team take on a tough op-

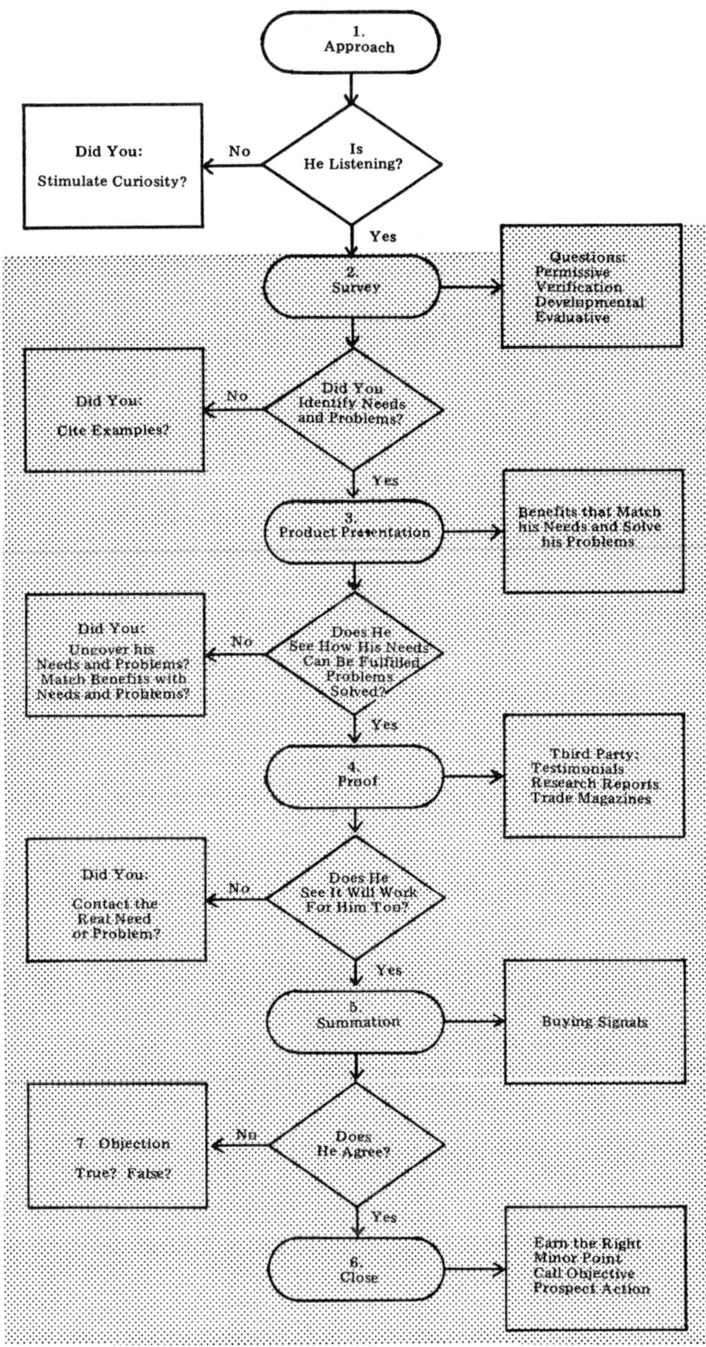

The Stages of the Sales Interview

ponent. During one of the tense moments, a complete stranger comes up to you and says "I just happened to be passing by and I thought I'd see if you'd be interested in our new Dingywampus" or "Here's something that you'll want to see" or "I want to sell you a . . ."

Often, that's the position in which you put your prospect. Oh, he's not watching a ball game, but he's engrossed in multiple business details or personal projects. A salesman is an interrupter of the day's routine; so the prospect gives you a few minutes. Remember, just because he gives you his *physical* presence does not mean you also have his *mental* presence.

People can concentrate on only one thing at a time. Interrupt them and they will continue to struggle with some remnants of their previous thoughts. In a sales interview, you have to keep that narrow, unsteady beam of attention focused on what you are saying. Once it begins to flicker, you're talking to yourself.

Without attention, your prospect will drift in and out of the interview. It's as if he came into the middle of a movie—he doesn't know if the cowboys are chasing the Indians or the Indians the cowboys! He will miss too much information to make an intelligent decision at the close. He knows it and, to be safe, he won't buy. However, we are concerned now with only the Approach. Once you proceed from the Approach to the Survey step, his attention is virtually guaranteed, as we shall see.

The problem is "How do you get his undivided attention at the very beginning?" This is the purpose—the only purpose—of the Approach.

It's a simple problem in economics. With many things competing for his attention, he's going to give his attention to those considerations that seem to promise the greatest return.

Here are some ideas that have worked well for me:

Introduction. Naturally, if this is a first-time call, you must introduce yourself and tell the prospect whom you represent. But keep it short. Your name isn't nearly as important to him as it is to you. Simply "Bill Jones with XYZ Company" will do. Your name and company doesn't become important until you prove by your interview that you are important to him. For the same reason, your business card is not important in the Approach. Give it to him when you say goodbye.

Amenities. If you must say, "I hope you are well," do it—it's important in some sections of the country and may be important for your personality. But keep discussion of the weather, the state of the man's business, "I haven't seen you for a long time," "I just happened by," etc., out of it. If you don't, you may lose your one chance of getting his attention. If the week's football game, business conditions, mutual friends seem important, discuss them *after* you make the sale.

Curiosity. This is a human trait universally distributed. Much of our learning from cradle to crypt is stimulated by the overwhelming need to know. Watch people in a social situation and observe how often actions are motivated by curiosity. A fire siren sends people running to find out where and what. A crowded sales table in a store stops the shopper. A new arrival at a party turns heads. The bang of a dropped book will silence 50 clattering typewriters. This being so, I have found these openers most effective:

- I have an idea for you.*
- I have something here that you couldn't possibly have seen before.
- I think I see a way that you can . . .
- A door-to-door salesman selling phonograph records of selections from the Bible says: "Do you have the voice of God in your home?"

Notice that no product is mentioned. Keep the name of your product out of the Approach (as well as the Survey). To mention your product is dangerous. The prospect, on hearing the product name, may say "I don't want any," or at least think it, and you've lost his attention.

Lead-in. Of course, you can discharge a shotgun and get attention, but it is difficult to bridge from this Approach to a discussion of your product! Don't burden yourself with such a dramatic opener that it takes two minutes of scrambling to get to your subject. The opener must be relevant to what you plan to say about your product.

Irrelevancies. As short and as simple as the Approach is, it is often the "catch pot" for multitudinous irrelevancies. As we have pointed out previously, the salesman is often a first-person-sensitive individual and, consequently, he feels a greater compulsion to impress his prospect, to get personal attention, to sound off on ex-

---

* From the book *The Fred Nauheim Nine-Day Sales Clinic* by Fred Nauheim. © 1964 by Prentice-Hall, Inc. Reprinted with permission.

traneous subjects than to proceed with the sale. I've accompanied some salesmen who have spent up to 85% of the available sales time in talking about irrelevancies and only 15% in talking about their product. If you think you must "warm up" your prospect, you are precisely the salesman I'm talking about. Recognize this problem for what it is. Irrelevancy is caused by your personality needs. Learn to subjugate them in the interests of selling more.

Keep It Short. The Approach should be no more than a few sentences long. If he's worth calling on, he's busy. Make time work for you, not against you. Many sales are lost, not because the prospect doesn't need the product or hasn't money to pay for it, but simply because the salesman talks too much.

Obviousness. Remember the purpose of the Approach—to get the undivided attention of the prospect. You won't do it with obviousness. "Undoubtedly, you have given some thought as to how you are going to provide a college education for your new son, haven't you?," starts an insurance salesman. This is too obvious and reflects no real thought given to the new father's position. "I have a plan that will enable Junior to go to college," elicits the *Ho Hum* reaction. Use your imagination. A better approach is, "Twenty years from now, only two high-school graduates out of ten will go to college. Will your son be one of them?"

Product Pamphlets and Information. Obviously, this is *not* the time to hand out the printed material on your product. For one thing, it will reveal your product. For another, it will distract the prospect's attention from what you are saying. Finally, he'll fiddle with it throughout the interview or become so engrossed in reading it he won't listen to you. If you use a pamphlet or book as a visualizer, be sure you retain control. Don't permit the prospect to pick it up and read through it during the interview.

Once you get the prospect's attention, move immediately into the Survey.

2. The Survey

WHERE YOU ARE

- At this time, you momentarily have the undivided attention of the prospect. He has a general feeling for the idea-pattern you are going to convey.

There are many variables in selling. Each prospect is one of a kind. One product is quite different in construction, utility, price, etc., from another (even in the same catalog). Every salesman has his own set of strengths and weaknesses. It is, then, particularly difficult to standardize the Survey Step (in fact, it should *not* be standardized). We must, therefore, content ourselves with the perimeters within which the salesman can operate.

STEP ONE:

First, ask either a Permissive Question or Verifying Question, depending on the circumstances. This is your "foot in the door."

STEP TWO:

Ask several Developmental Questions. Here's how you decide what questions to ask:

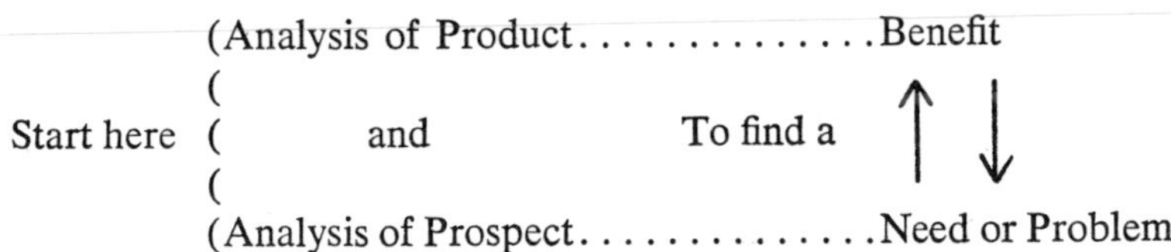

Because you have complete knowledge of your product and probably only suspicions or tentative assumptions about your prospect, proceed to learn more about the prospect within the framework of the needs fulfilled or problems solved by your product.

Traditionally, a product presentation is made in this sequence:

(1) Product feature ⟶ (2) Prospect benefit ⟶ (3) Need fulfilled

Of course, some salesmen fail to convert product features into prospect benefits and still fewer make any reference to the prospect needs that are fulfilled. Thus, they lose one of the more fruitful opportunities to sell. Begin by thinking through each feature to find the need or the problem it is designed to fulfill or solve. Then, reverse your thinking:

(1) What are the needs? ⟶ (2) How will the prospect benefit? ⟶ (3) What feature is important?

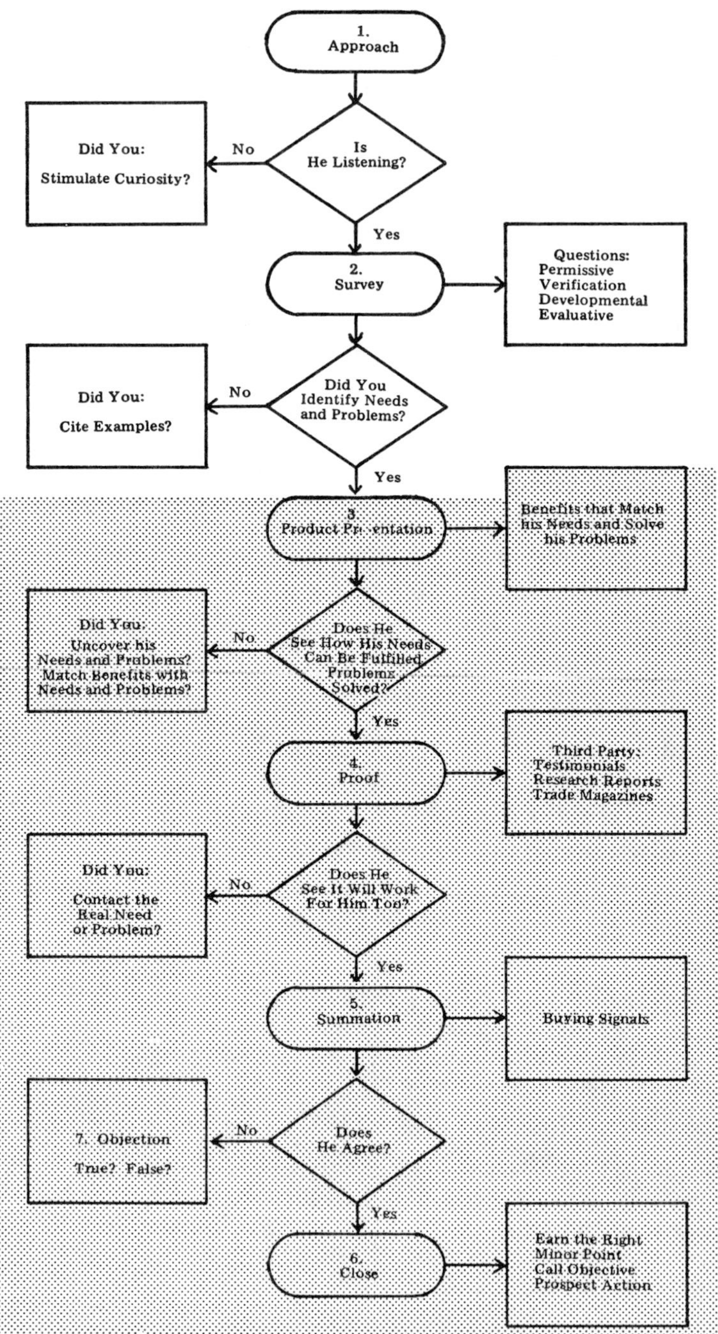

The Stages of the Sales Interview

Of course, (1) What are his needs? is the only consideration pertinent to the survey. In the Product Presentation, you present (2) (How will he benefit?) and (3) (What feature is important?).

Traditional . . . (Little or no information on prospect).

(1)	(2)	(3)
Feature →	Benefit →	Needs or Problem
Nylon gear	No lubrication	Little or no preventive maintenance

Survey .... (prospect works on a small margin)

(1)	(2)	(3)
Needs →	Benefit * →	Feature *
If I could show you a program that would virtually eliminate downtime and cost of preventive maintenance, would you be interested?	Nylon gears have a low coefficient of friction and require no lubrication.	Our Dingywampus has nylon gears in all critical retroactive positions.

* Use in Product Presentation (not in Survey).

Usually, you will use the Survey only to determine (1) Needs. You will want to accumulate several needs (as in the Benton-McTavish interview) during the Survey.

STEP THREE:

Once you feel your case is strong enough (you have uncovered several needs or identified a problem), you ask an Evaluative Question, which does nothing more than summarize the needs and isolate the problem. It directs the prospect's thoughts to the Product Presentation that will follow.

HERE'S WHERE WE ARE

We have advanced through Stage 1, Approach, and Stage 2, Survey. Let's stop here while I give you an example of these two stages.

HARDWARE JOBBER SALESMAN— HARDWARE-LUMBER-YARD OWNER *

SALESMAN:	Good morning, Mr. Bishop. I'm Bill Stone with Belmont Hardware. We met at the Hardware Show in Kansas City last month.	
OWNER:	Yes. I remember you. Great show wasn't it?	
SALESMAN:	Yes indeed. You were kind enough to stop at our booth and inspect our new department merchandising unit. I'm eager to get your impressions. Is it OK to ask a few questions?	Permissive Q:
OWNER:	Sure, but I'm not sure my opinion is too important. You see I'm kind of new at hardware merchandising. I was a contractor up to ten months ago.	Probably knows tools, quality, wearing abilities.
SALESMAN:	Then I assume you are an expert on tools and power equipment? And can I also assume that you might be interested in various methods of hardware merchandising?	Verifying Q:
OWNER:	Absolutely. However I haven't much money to spend with getting the business started and all.	Wants help in merchandising. Short of money?
SALESMAN:	Tell me. What does a carpenter or contractor look for in . . . say, a power saw?	Developmental Q:

Following a series of Developmental Questions, Bill accumulates this information:

1. Bishop may be short of money.
2. Knows very little about merchandising.
3. Recognizes and can sell quality power equipment.
4. Has "tie-in" with local Contractors' Association.

---

* H. B. Rames, *Synergistic Selling* (Lincoln, Nebr.: Panel Book, Springboard Assoc., 1971), pp. 26–27.

SALESMAN: Mr. Bishop, at this point, am I correct in assuming that if I can show you a plan that will: number one, do an excellent job of merchandising power equipment and give you a turnover 6 times a year; number two, include only the top triple-X quality Tigerline; number three, give you a mark-up high enough that you can give the usual contractor's discount and still make 25% profit and, finally, be purchased on a 90-day dating—if I can do this—will you be interested? — Evaluation Q

The hardware-jobber salesman's Survey was structured as follows:

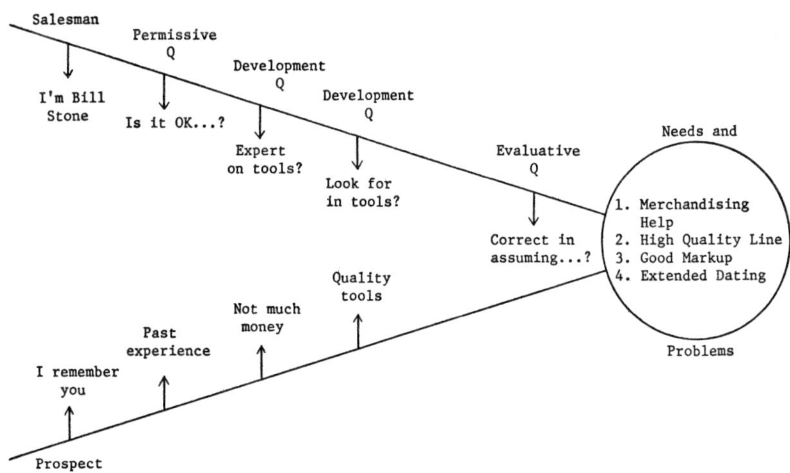

The Survey extracts information from the prospect that determines what needs the salesman's product must satisfy to make a sale. It's all done with questions that allow the prospect to participate and encourage him to think through to his problems.

The Survey requires more thinking and planning at the beginning; but once you have used it several times, it becomes a habit that's easily followed. Remember the first time you rode a bicycle or drove a car?

10

How to Mobilize the Magic of Heads-Up Negotiating in Dynamic Sales Interviews

Negotiation is human behavior in action. Whenever people meet together—from the United Nations to a salesman and his client—ideas are exchanged and agreements are made. Underlying it all are personal needs to be met and problems to be solved.

Until a few years ago, there were no reliable guidelines for effective negotiation. The procedures were based on trial and error. Now, thanks to the exhaustive research done in the behavioral sciences, one fact recurs with regular frequency. *It is the negotiator who has a knowledge of human behavior who emerges successful.* Each party to a negotiation has needs. When the negotiator chooses to ignore the needs of the other party, when he wants to *win* and wants the other party to *lose,* an agreement cannot be reached! Athletic contests may be conducted on a win-or-lose basis, but in negotiation, both parties must win or there can be no agreement. Central to "heads-up" negotiation is the anticipation and the satisfaction of human needs for *both* parties to the negotiation.

Let's see how this basic principle applies to sales negotiations, as we pick up our analysis of the sales interview where we left it in Chapter 9.

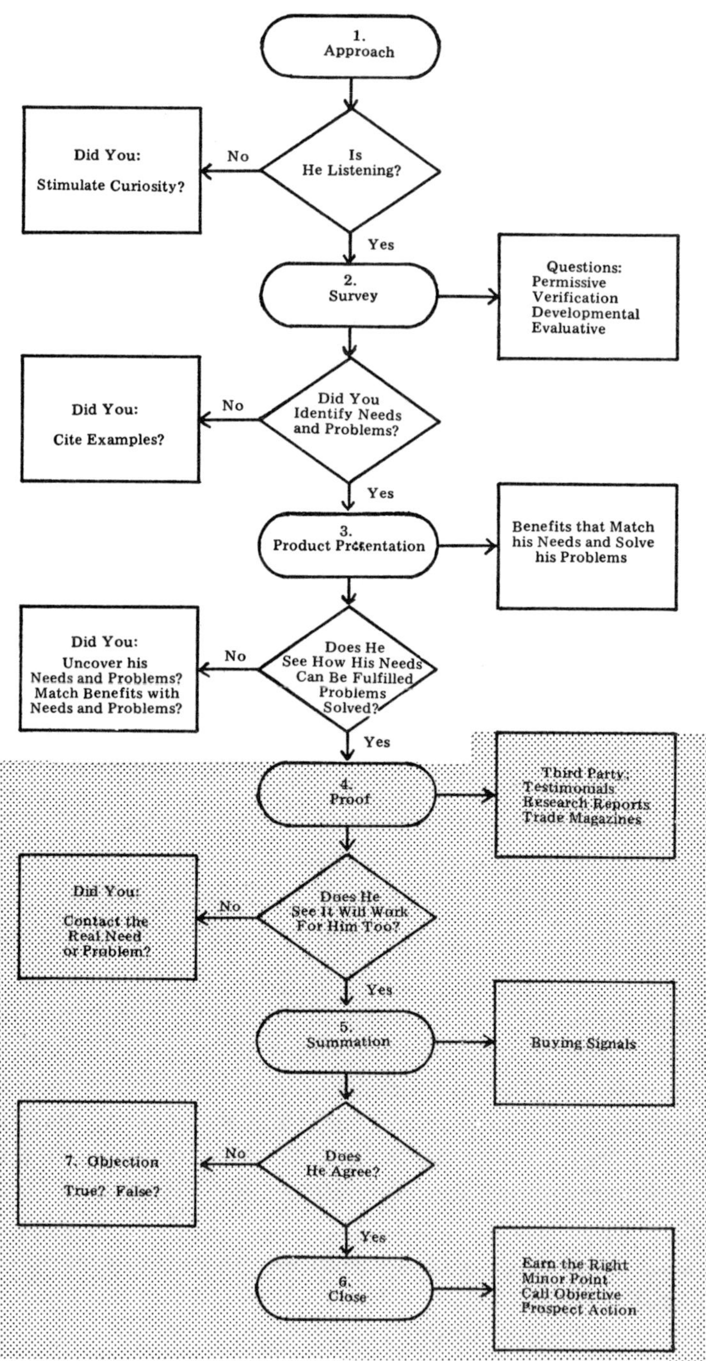

The Stages of the Sales Interview

3. The Product Presentation

WHERE YOU ARE

• At this time you have retained attention and fanned interest through prospect participation.

• At this time you have a fairly good grasp of the prospect's personal motivations or needs.

• At this time you probably have isolated a problem for which your product offers a solution.

The Product Presentation should offer no difficulties to you. However, you may have to school yourself to:

1. Emphasize prospect *benefits* first, instead of product features.
2. Emphasize only those benefits (followed by supporting product features) that match the needs disclosed in the Survey.

The Product Presentation follows this sequence:

(1)	(2)	(3)
Need	Prospect Benefit	Product Feature
(Previously uncovered and emphasized in Evaluative Question)	Example: Maintenance is reduced by 25% because of	the extra filter of our XY model

Trial Close. Despite the care with which you explored for the prospect's need in the Survey Stage, you are not always absolutely sure that the need is valid, nor that he feels the benefit-feature is an important one. So you simply ask him, for instance: "Is this a valuable saving to you, Mr. Prospect?" This is called a Trial Close. The answer tells you where he stands on the subject. If he does not respond in an affirmative manner, he either has not understood or the need does not exist in any strength. You may wish to explain it more thoroughly or simply move on to another need.

A Trial Close has another benefit to you: It breaks up a long message into smaller, more digestible bits. Jesse S. Nirenberg, an industrial psychologist says, "If you are trying to educate or influence others you oughtn't to speak for more than about 20 seconds at any one time. Your listener can't absorb any more than this in one bite." *

Objectivity. I told you that the Product Presentation in Synergistic Selling would be shorter and simpler. Here's why: A prospect does not buy because of the sheer weight of many benefits. He buys because one or two or three benefits appear important to him (they match his needs). Reciting benefits in which he has no interest needlessly burdens the sales interview. Actually, we have found that mentioning extraneous benefits is a dangerous procedure. He may respond, "Oh, your Dingywampus has a flimflam on the leading edge? Then I don't want it. Sorry. Had one once. Never liked it."

Be objective. You uncovered needs in the Survey. Stay with these needs. If all of them go sour on you, then you didn't conduct your Survey properly. So return to the Survey and repeat it in hopes that you can now uncover the *real* needs.

Returning to the Survey is relatively easy. Stop and say something like this:

> Mr. Prospect, may I impose on you for a few more minutes? Several weeks ago, I called on a company in the eastern part of the state quite similar to yours in many respects. The Production Manager had . . . *(explore a problem or need that you suspect the prospect has).*

You rekindle his interest with a story! The Greatest Teacher of them all used stories to illustrate a point—why not you? You're back on track. Try again to uncover his need. He has now been sensitized to the need and may be more receptive to your urging to explore for it.

During the Product Presentation, you will probably score several points as the prospect senses how his psychological needs can be fulfilled or as you explain how his problem can be solved. It is also possible that some needs or problems prove to be less important to him and are discarded.

A temptation that some salesmen succumb to at this time is to

---

*From the book, *Getting Through to People* by J. Nirenberg. © 1968 by Prentice-Hall, Inc. Reprinted with permission.

try to close. Interest is high. The prospect may have given you buying signals. Closing action is desirable and often successful at this point—*but only if you are confident of a firm match of needs with benefits.* When your position is strong, try to close. If unsuccessful, all is not lost; merely return to Step 4. When buying signals are absent, advance to Step 4.

4. Proof

WHERE YOU ARE

• At this time you have a match between several prospect needs and product benefits.

• Furthermore, you have obtained agreement from prospect that he recognizes this relationship.

The Proof is a simple step, so simple, in fact, that it is often omitted and, as a result, the sale suffers. The prospect may have agreed with you in principle that a need can be filled and a problem solved with your product. But remember, you are trying to effect change, and people are not quick to change even when they see it's to their advantage to do so. They change slowly and only when they become accustomed to the notion that most of the risk of change doesn't exist.

Prospects Are Skeptical. Prospects doubt the accuracy of their own judgment. ("What if I am wrong? How will I defend my judgment to my boss or wife?" etc.) Then too, many people are suspicious of salesmen. ("He's a smooth talker—too smooth. I'm silly to follow his partisan advice," etc.) Clearly, this is a situation in which a third party's advice and counsel would be helpful.

You supply third-party advice in the form of testimonials, research, reports, news items from trade magazines and the comments of satisfied customers or experts whose opinions are reliable. This is a good place for a demonstration if you have one.

Many salesmen present the company pamphlet or catalog at this time, pointing out a graph, picture or claim that is made. This is the best place for such materials; however, be sure to use it for a purpose. Let it add to your presentation, not detract from it.

Only prove the benefits that your Product Presentation has shown to be important. The prospect has clearly indicated that he isn't

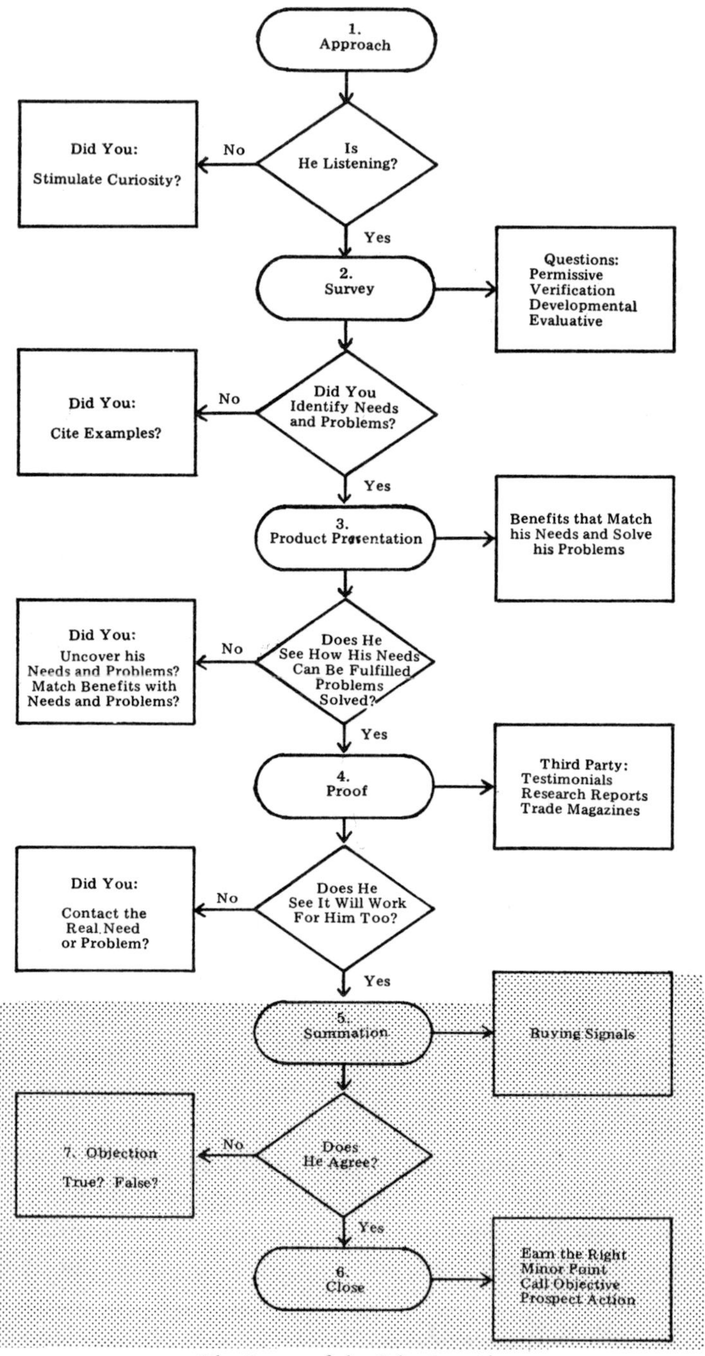

The Stages of the Sales Interview

interested in some benefits, no matter how important *you* think they are. Prove only those need satisfactions or problem solutions that are important to this particular prospect.

Several months ago, a salesman presented me with a notebook full of testimonial letters. "Just skim through *that,*" he said. "We have many satisfied customers." There must have been 150 letters from all over the country! I wasn't as impressed with this dog-eared collection of nothing as I would have been with one letter from a reputable firm telling of their experience with the product in a situation similar to mine.

How to Express It. As you present your proof, do so with words to this effect: "To illustrate the (benefit) of the XL Dingywampus, here is (a report from the XX State University Research Center), which stresses the (benefit) by pointing out . . ." Don't use the argumentative words, "Here's proof of (what I say is true)."

Give Him Time. Salesmen abhor silence. While the prospect is busily engaged in doing the one thing he wants him to do—thinking—the salesman, eager for the kill, breaks the sound barrier and speaks. Remember, silence is golden; and it can be just that to you. Give the prospect time to think. Underscore the important points in your proof. A testimonial letter, a research report or a trade magazine news item frequently has a lot of soggy words in it, with only one or two pertinent sentences. Underline these sentences so that the prospect's eyes will immediately fall on those sentences. Don't require the prospect to read the entire report.

Questions and Objections. I have found that Synergistic Selling eliminates most difficult objections. However, some do remain. They will be discussed later in this chapter. At this stage of the interview, and in the next stage, there will be questions and objections as the prospect begins to come to a decision.

Recycle. If questions and objections indicate that the prospect is not with you, it usually means that you did not uncover the real needs of the prospect. To save the sale, it is necessary for you to recycle your interview through the Survey Stage. This is not a difficult task because by this time he has had more time to consider his needs and problems. Something like this will reintroduce the Survey:

> Mr. Prospect, at this time, I am not quite sure how you view an improved system of air conditioning. Do you have the kind of store that can generate more customers next summer as a consequence of an improved system?

This is sometimes called "negative sell." This switch in technique may stimulate the prospect to "qualify" himself, to prove to you that he does have needs and can use your product.

Advance. When the Proof Stage indicates that the prospect is with you and questions have been answered to his satisfaction, it is necessary to move into the Summation and Close.

5. The Summation

WHERE YOU ARE

- At this time you have isolated several needs and problems. You have matched them with benefit-features.
- At this time you have satisfactorily used third-party proof to support each benefit that the prospect feels is important.

In a court of law, it is customary for attorneys to bring into sharp focus the important details of the case prior to asking the jury to come to a decision. Thus, jury members, who may be predisposed to one verdict or another, are exposed to an abbreviated description of the case, which interprets the pros and cons. It compels the jury members to review, to reconsider, to compare. It points their thinking in the direction of a decision.

The summation in a sales interview serves a similar purpose. It serves also as a bridge between discussion and decision—easing the tension for both prospect and salesman. It allows you to create *your own opportunity to close.*

EXAMPLES:

> You have told me you have a need to save money or a problem of reducing rejects, (etc.). I have explained how Dingywampus offers an (economical) way to solve this problem through its (benefit). Before we go on, do you have any further questions?

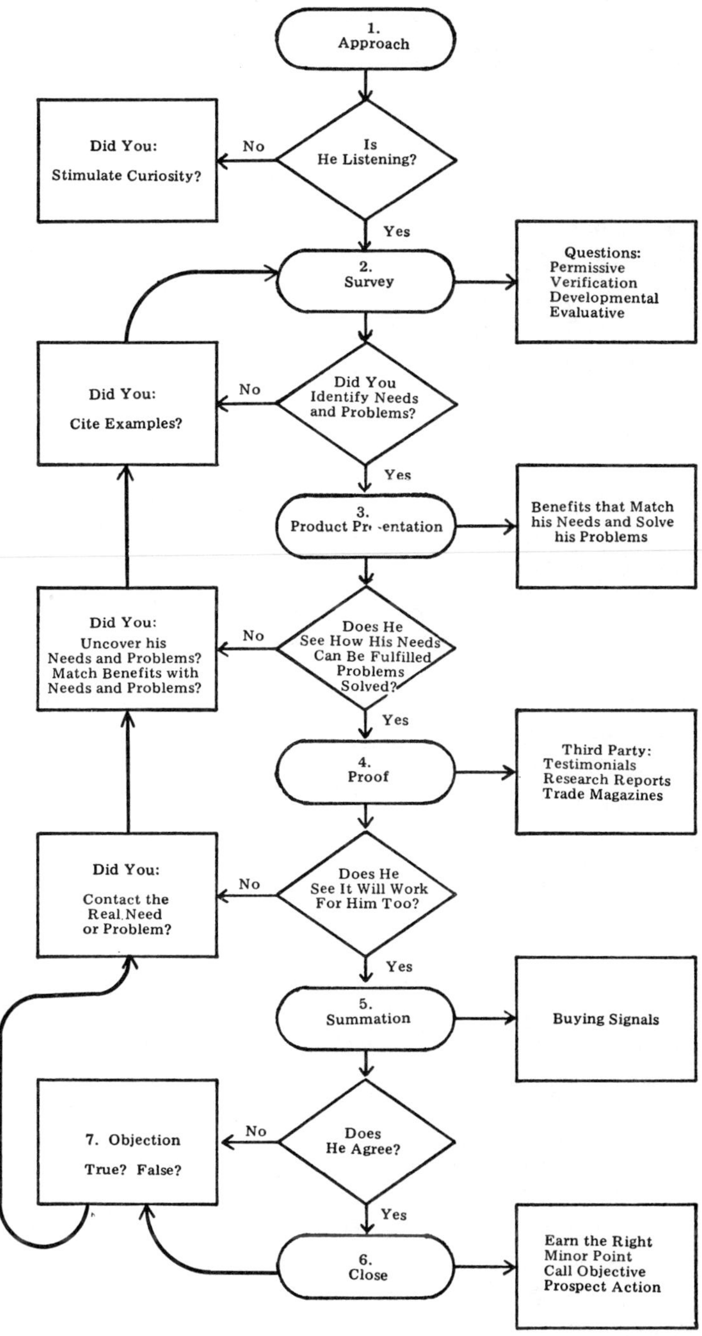

The Stages of the Sales Interview

If a non-negotiable consideration such as price or delivery has the potential of barring the sale:

> Is there any reason, other than money, delivery, (etc.), that will prevent you from going ahead at this time?

Buying Signals. Often, the prospect will unknowingly provide you with an opportunity to close. He does so with buying signals. When they are present, it is not necessary to summate. Such a signal might be his questions, "Do you have it in green?"; "How soon can I get delivery?"

6. The Close

Traditionally, the toughest stage of selling is the close. However, this is not the case when the Dynamic Laws are used effectively.

Someone once said that the big problem with an automated sales presentation is that the customer hasn't memorized his lines! This certainly applies to the close; for he never seems to recognize his cue to say "Yes."

Analyses of both conventional sales presentations and synergistic sales interviews reveal that about 80% of each are never closed; but there the similarity ends. Although the salesman practicing the Dynamic Laws does not always go through an actual closing action, he frequently gets the order. Simply stated, the prospect decides to buy before it is necessary to resort to a closing action. The reason? Because he recognizes the match between need (or problem) and product—a match that *you* have helped him to arrive at.

In the conventional sales presentation, closing action is often not taken simply because it is a very difficult step for the average salesman. He skirts around the issue by asking, "Are there any more questions?" when he should be asking "How should we move ahead on this?" He is probably a first-person-sensitive individual. He wants to preserve his self-respect. A "No" or "I'll think about it" is ego-damaging. The conventional close is so difficult and so few salesmen are willing to subject themselves to the potential damage, that sales managers and sales consultants have for years advocated that we "change the salesman or change the sales job."

The Dynamic Laws change both the salesman, by causing him to be more empathetic toward the needs of the prospect, and the sales job, by making it unnecessary to employ strong closing action.

Earn the Right to Close. You severely handicap yourself and the success of closing action if you haven't identified the needs and problems on which the success of the close depends. These are so fundamental that this point can scarcely be overemphasized. Earn the right to close during the Survey, Presentation and Proof, and enter the Close with deserved confidence that you will be successful.

Minor-Point Close. When the prospect does not voluntarily agree to buy (during Stages 3, 4, or 5), the mildest of closing actions is all that is required. I have found the Minor-Point Close to be generally successful. It is a form of Assumptive Close that asks the prospect to make his choice among minor considerations (color, delivery, credit terms, models, styles, etc.).

> Which plan, the gross offer with an extra 15% discount or the six dozen offer with a 10% discount, will satisfy your profit requirements at this time?
>
> Would you prefer to give me a check today or shall we ship with delivery charges collect?

You can use several Minor-Point Closes without appearing to be high-pressure.

If you submit written orders, you can ask such minor-point questions while completing the order. Incidentally, you should bring your order book out during the Summation to get the prospect accustomed to seeing it. Open it during the Minor-Point Close and begin to enter the information.

Call Objective. A critical factor in making some types of sales is to have a call objective. This is especially important if you are a detail man—a salesman who solicits business but does not actually write an order (a pharmaceutical salesman, for instance). Without a call objective, it is easy for the prospect to avoid making a decision by merely saying, "I'll think about it" or "I'll try to remember it." Such a statement is not a strong enough commitment to constitute a successful close.

A call objective is a specific request for a certain prospect action, which has a precise time limitation. Decide which of the following statements qualify as call objectives:

1. To sell him on my company.
2. To get him to approve an order for shipping one dozen Dingywampus this month.
3. To get acquainted. To sell myself.
4. To get him to agree to a trial of Product X on the next ten patients.
5. To sell him on the new Expandex system.
6. To get him to allow us to make a office layout study next week.

Only the even-numbered statements comply with the requirements for a call objective. A salesman who calls for reasons in the odd-numbered statements cannot close short of saying, "Will you buy today?," which is amateurish and ineffective. Consequently, each "sales call" becomes a social visit—nothing more.

A call objective is very useful in those situations that reasonably require more than one call to make the sale. In the cases where a husband must talk to his wife about life insurance or in a "big-ticket" item such as new furniture for an entire office, the salesmen must decide on a call objective for each call.

For instance, a salesman selling an insurance-stock retirement program may plot his call objectives in this way:

Sales Call No.	Selling Action	Call Objective
1.	Stimulate interest in insurance-stock retirement program.	Let us survey present insurance and stock holdings.
2.	Report on projected income of present holdings. Inform on effect of inflation.	Get husband and wife to agree on desired income level in relation to anticipated inflation.
3.	Closing action.	Agree to signing application for X dollars.

By having a call objective for each step, you gradually but surely advance to the successful close: You close in stages. This is an excellent way to sell a big proposition because it does not require the prospect to make a big decision—merely several small decisions. People are more inclined to accept a major change when it is presented in small steps with time to think and get accustomed to the idea between the steps.

A Close is a Question. Elementary as it seems, some salesmen avoid closing with a question. It's as if they didn't want to close—as if they wanted to keep the negotiation in limbo for eternity! Such statements as "We have many satisfied customers" or "We give fast service" are not closes. They are calculated to keep the prospect comfortable. Yet a mild degree of discomfort is necessary—just enough so that when he decides to go ahead, he feels relieved.

Prospect Action. I have found that in those types of selling that do not require a specific prospect action (such as signing an order), it is well to create or synthesize a prospect action. For example, one of the firms I have worked with has a sales force that solicits dealers to sell a service to industrial firms. Obviously, there is no inventory and no prospect action. The firm's salesmen could get an agreement from a potential dealer that he would promote the service; but many failed to perform. We changed the Close to specify a call objective that required prospect action merely by supplying a window decal to the salesmen. The decal stated that the dealer was an agent for XYZ Company. Then the salesman, after getting agreement from the dealer, tried to fulfill his call objective through prospect action by using a minor-point close: "Where shall we put this decal, on the front door or on the window?" This has the effect of firming up a personal commitment of the dealer's true intentions and isolating those dealers who might require further persuasion.

If there is no prospect action in your Close, try to create one in the form of something the prospect must do physically at that precise time. A completed physical action is *prima facie* evidence that you have closed the sale.

THE CLOSE AND THE DYNAMIC SALES LAWS

• The Dynamic Laws allow you to close the easy way—the thinking salesman's way.

- Earn the right to close by identifying the prospect's needs and problems on which the Close depends.
- When the Dynamic Laws have been observed, all you need is a gentle decision-making technique, the Minor-Point Close, to make the sale.
- Enter each sales call with a firm Call Objective.
- Remember that a Close is a Question.
- Try for Prospect Action in the Close.

7. The Objection

Objections do not constitute a stage in the sales interview; for they can occur at any time. Most frequently, they are voiced between Stages 4 (Proof) and 6 (Close), because the prospect senses that he will soon be required to make a decision.

The Dynamic Laws minimize both the number of objections and their severity, because the focus is on the prospect—his needs and problems—with which he finds little to disagree.

For our ease in discussing objections, they may be classified into:

1. The question—a request for more information.
2. The true objection.
3. The false objection.

I know of no analysis that has been made to determine the distribution of objections into these groups; but I would estimate that, of the total, 40% would fall into class 1—requests for more information—whether the request is made in the form of a question or an objection. Another 40% would be considered false objections and only 20% are true objections. Such an estimate, which seems realistic to my experience, tends to reduce the problem of objections to a manageable level.

Three-Step Formula. Fundamental to dealing with objections is listening and observing carefully—even if you believe you know what the prospect is objecting to. You can learn a lot about the prospect in what he objects to, how he expresses himself, his posture, mannerisms and gestures. Is he emphatic? Sure of himself? Does he supply evidence to support his position? Is he rather apologetic, timid? Is he testing you? Does he speak spontaneously or only after careful consideration?

Now follow this sequence:

STEP 1. DECIDE WHETHER OR NOT YOU UNDERSTAND THE OBJECTION

If you do not understand:

Never try to answer an objection you don't understand. If you don't understand, say something like this: "Let's see if I understand your position, Mr. Prospect. You asked (rephrase his question). Is that correct?" It may be that you'll have to ask additional questions. This is very much a part of negotiation. It allows your prospect to re-examine his position and gives you time to think. He may decide not to defend his position after all.

If you understand:

Go to Step 2.

STEP 2. DECIDE IF OBJECTION IS TRUE OR FALSE

If false:

Many objections are stalls, e.g., "I've got to talk to my wife." "I haven't got the money." "I'll think about it," etc. These are simply excuses for deferring action. Should you acknowledge them by trying to answer them, the prospect's strategy will become reinforced. Actually, these questions are very difficult to answer because they have so little substance. So you ignore them and keep on selling, like this:

PROSPECT: I haven't got the money.
SALESMAN: Ok, now here's another advantage . . .

If the objection is brought into the conversation again, you can assume that it may hold some truth and you should try to get more information by asking questions of the prospect. Other objections, called "smoke screens," can also be considered false, e.g., "I understand your competition lowered their price last week." "I've never had a call for your product," etc.

Prospects who habitually bring up false objections generally must be closed harder than prospects who are not addicted to stalls and smoke screens. For one reason or another, "false-objections prospects" have lost confidence in their own judgment. You must actively help them to arrive at decisions.

If true:

If the objection has the ring of validity in it, go to Step 3.

STEP 3. ANSWER OBJECTION

You are now dealing with a true objection. As a matter of attitude, think of it as a question—a request for more information.

Concede. The major problem that occurs in answering objections is the win–or–lose concept that exists. Obviously, both prospect and salesman want to win and, consequently, either one or both get defensive at this time. You can find the middle ground of agreement by conceding that the question is a good one. "You have presented an interesting problem" or "I can certainly appreciate your position" or "I agree that is an important point to discuss before proceeding." By conceding, you take the "sting" out of the rebuttal and set the stage for a sensible discussion. You are not surrendering your position.

More Information. Many times, it is good technique to get the prospect to talk more about his position. A simple question will do it: "Let's see if I understand. You said. . . Is that correct?" With this maneuver you may uncover some needs and problems not exposed during your Survey.

Understanding. Let him know you understand. "In other words, you ask if Dingywampus won't (reduce the severity of the objection). Here, let me illustrate with this report from . . ." You are, in effect, recycling through the sales interview with a Third-Party Reference.

During this step, it may be wise to refer to the needs and problems originally identified in the Survey. A personal need, when satisfied, will often overshadow a minor objection.

Trial Close. Now you must determine if you have satisfied his question. "I'm glad you brought this up. Does this new information help?"

Summate and Close. If the objection occurred during the final stages of the interview, you have merely made a detour. However, you are now back "on track," and it will be necessary to summate and close again.

PRICE OBJECTIONS

Delay Price Question. When a price question or objection occurs early in the interview, it is probably not wise to answer it until you uncover needs and match them with product benefits (because the price will always be "too much"). Simply reply "If you don't mind, I'll answer that in just a minute."

Lead Him Away. When a price question occurs later in the interview, it is well to lead him away from price unless you feel that he has a good grasp of the benefits.

PROSPECT: How much?
SALESMAN: An important consideration, Mr. Prospect. Tell me how many years do you figure you'll be using (the product)?
PROSPECT: Oh, about five years.
SALESMAN: Then quality and dependability are of utmost importance. Let me show you why Dingywampus is such a good buy. The geer and spindle assembly is . . . The complete system is priced at X dollars.

Break Cost Into Smaller Increments. When the price becomes important later in the interview, break it up into smaller increments.

PROSPECT: What's it cost?
SALESMAN: Five-hundred dollars.
PROSPECT: Oh brother! I can't afford that. Why, your competitor priced their product at $427.50.
SALESMAN: Let's look at it this way. You told me you wanted (remind him of his needs or problems) and that you expected to use it for five years. Dingywampus will allow you to enjoy its extra benefits at less than fifteen dollars a year. Isn't the added value to you worth fifteen dollars?

Avoid Making Price the Determining Factor. Don't let price become a major obstacle to completion of the sale. Historically, prospects have found the price objection so effective that they frequently fall back upon it. To most salesmen this problem is insurmountable, unless they learn how to turn the conversation to a strong selling point.

PROSPECT: Your price is too high.
SALESMAN: Aside from price, do you find any other serious criticism, Mr. Prospect?
PROSPECT: No, I guess not. The product is good. I like this feature and that . . . etc.
SALESMAN: Let me show you how you'll actually save money with these features . . .

Using Objections to Close

Many alert salesmen use objections or questions as a close. For example:

PROSPECT: How soon could I get a car like this?
SALESMAN: How soon do you want it?

The prospect's answer can commit him. This is the only closing action required. The salesman merely starts to write the order.

PROSPECT: Do the drapes come with the house?
SALESMAN: Do you want them to come with the house?

PROSPECT: $1,995 and my old car? I didn't expect to pay more than $1,850.
SALESMAN: If I can get your price, will you buy?

PROSPECT: If I give you an order, how soon can I expect delivery?
SALESMAN: How soon do you want it?
(No matter what figure the prospect mentions, the salesman starts to write the order.)

Thus, we see how the effective use of the Dynamic Laws throughout the stages of the sales interview can lead to a successful close. The salesman must be observant, questioning and positive in his efforts to make the prospect recognize the ways in which his needs or problems can be solved by the product. Keeping this in mind, the application of these principles will lead you to greater achievements in motivating your prospects to buy.

11

How to Apply the Dynamic Laws to Your Tough Prospects

You now have a workable knowledge of perception and the application of the Technique of Questioning throughout the sales interview. At this time, it will be useful to examine a simplified method of classifying prospect reactions so that you can quickly adopt the sales style most effective for making the sale in each specific instance.

Our objective in this chapter will be to examine and classify prospect reactions, to determine the basic needs behind the reactions and to decide on a sales strategy most appropriate to each.

Prospect Reactions: Surface Signals of Inner Needs

A physician who treats the pain and discomfort of pneumonia, but ignores the infection, might be called a quack or a charlatan (or worse). Physicians, through training and experience, become adept at classifying symptoms and, from them, deducing what disorders they represent. They then proceed to treat the disease, knowing that, as the disease is brought under control, the symptoms will disappear.

Little progress can be made in medicine—or sales—when we persist in treating symptoms; but we do this far too often in sales. When a prospect is belligerent, do you look for the underlying cause? No. We fight fire with fire and, as a consequence, we have *two* belligerent people where before we had only one. When a prospect is quiet and unresponsive, do we pause to consider what this reaction means? No. We try to arouse enthusiasm in him by talking louder and even exaggerating the presentation.

Prospect reactions, like physical symptoms, are only surface manifestations of inner needs and problems. Be grateful that they exist, because they make it easier for you to perceive those needs that they represent.

Personal Needs—the Basis for Sales Motivation

Earlier, we reviewed the Pyramid of Needs—a working theory of motivation, which maintains that everybody's motivation is somewhere on the continuum between physical needs at the one extreme and self-actualization at the other. Furthermore, we are continually changing; for as one set of needs is fulfilled, another set emerges to take its place. Thus, we see that people are constantly being motivated to satisfy their needs throughout life.

Here is another statement of needs, which is not as classical but sometimes more useful. It simplifies the classification into Physical, Social and Egoistic needs.

Classification of Basic Needs That Determine Behavior

1. PHYSICAL NEEDS

These are the familiar needs of food, water, air, temperature control, shelter, clothing and sleep. These needs, as motivators of behavior, are most often observed in the infant.

2. SOCIAL NEEDS

These are needs that find an end product in a particular relationship with other people.

a. Affiliation—the need to associate with other people, to be a member, to be accepted. This need explains fraternities in college, trade associations in business, informal work groups in industry, etc.

b. Affection—the need to be liked. Loyalty to a company, a college or a family is an example of affection needs.

3. EGOISTIC NEEDS

These needs are not related to others, but to oneself. Egoistic needs strive toward recognition, status, telling others what to do, etc. The great drive to personal achievement, which spurs many a man in business, is essentially an egoistic need. The accumulation of wealth, a big home, a large wardrobe, etc., are classified here, as is the desire for autonomy. The need for information is also an egoistic need.

Take a little time to think about your product. What needs does it fulfill? Why do people buy it? Don't be satisfied with the superficial comment, "Because they need it." Why do they need it? Does it satisfy a physical need? A social need? No matter what product you're selling, chances are good that it fills an egoistic need. This is a need that pertains to oneself, but is not necessarily selfish.

Needs are important because they give rise to the reactions of prospects—the subject of this chapter.

Select Your Sales Strategy

My old friend, Elmer Wheeler, used to have a bunch of corny old phrases such as "Say it with flowers," and "Don't write, telegraph." There's absolutely nothing wrong with corn: It makes whiskey, provides millions of dollars in tax revenue to the Federal Government, and provides food and employment to countless people. Never underestimate the value of corn or its adjective, corny—people love it!

What Elmer was trying to get salesmen to accept was the use of a strategy that has sparkle with people who have a psychological need for it. Thus, flowers say "thank you" to people who need to be accepted, to be liked for what they are. A telegram says to the prospect who is striving for esteem, "I think you're important." These are the magic and wonderful things that we can do to "change the complexion of the day."

This applies, in a very practical sense, to selling. You may not send flowers or telegrams, but by observing reactions and deciding on the inner needs they represent, you can use a particular sales style; you can abbreviate the interview or lengthen it; you can select the right benefit; you can stress one sales step over another; you can avoid sensitive areas. In short, you can help fulfill a need, solve a problem and make the sale. That's the strategy!

We are going to talk about prospect reactions as if they were actual prospects because it's easier to think of them that way. This material is modified from my programmed textbook, *Synergistic Selling.*

Prospect #1
Jack Armstrong, the All-American Prospect

Jack is the average prospect. He, like most of us, is made up of many different characteristics—some good, some bad, many indifferent. All are subject to change, depending on conditions, state of readiness, mental set, etc.

We generally think of ourselves as being fairly astute buyers. (We aren't really. Look around your home at the many things you have that you don't really need and wonder why you bought!) We frequently argue with a salesman that, "It's a good deal, but I just haven't the money." We are adept at the smoke screen, "I'm just looking around. I probably won't buy until the fall." In reality, we don't like the way the salesman talks to us or we don't like his manner. If we would only look deeper, we'd realize that he didn't compliment us by pushing the right button—the button labeled "Need" or "Want."

Yes, Jack Armstrong is like most of us. He'll pick on some little point of vulnerability in your sales story and build up a big case out of it. It's not an important point to him really—just his defense against buying. Often, his defense is price.

He's not difficult; he's just human, like you and me. We as salesmen get into difficulty when we don't think of him as a person—a person constantly responding to needs and wants. When we allow him to participate in the interview, when we uncover his wants and appeal to them, he will tend to buy. Wouldn't you?

How to Tailor Your Sales Interview

You must have a reason for calling on Jack. This reason can't be that you have something to sell him; rather, it must be that you have an idea (not a product) to present that will help him to satisfy his needs, reach his goals or maintan his self-image of importance. Jack Armstrong will buy such an idea, whereas he will not buy merely a product.

"I have an idea for you today. But first, so that its application to your situation can be clearly stated, may I ask a few questions?" Such an approach will gain the immediate and undivided attention of Jack Armstrong because it invites his participation.

"Mr. Armstrong, first may I ask if you are acquainted with Belmont Estates?" Such a Verifying Question states your purpose in calling. Mr. Armstrong's response indicates his state of readiness.

Before mid-point in the typical prospect-oriented interview, you might ask, "What returns do you look for in a real estate investment, Mr. Armstrong?" A Developmental Question such as this gives direction to what needs must be satisfied in order to sell him.

After a short presentation of the benefits of your proposal, which appeals to Mr. Armstrong, any critical questions or requests for further information can be easily handled because his investment requirements are now known to you. He remains responsive and cooperative because your entire interview is centered around *his* interests.

You entered the interview with a call objective—possibly to have him accept your invitation to inspect Belmont Estates. This is all you try to "sell" on this call. Thus, at no time does Jack feel that he is being pressured.

VIVE LA DIFFERENCE

Fortunately, most prospects are "Jack Armstrongs" most of the time. When they are not, you must sense the change; you must observe the reactions that signal the necessity to employ a different sales strategy. Some prospects are never Jack Armstrongs but react consistently in an "offbeat" fashion.

Most salesmen can sell a reasonable amount of merchandise to Jack Armstrong; but they never get rich until they learn to sell when reactions are less favorable. It's selling in the face of reactions that are different from the average that is the badge of good salesmanship.

When dealing with the offbeat prospect, here is the encouraging note: When prospects react differently, this difference is their vulnerable spot—their Achilles heel! It involves their special needs, their self-image, their goals, their problems. Disregard it, fight it and you won't sell much. Recognize it, make favorable contact with it and you can sell in the face of unfavorable reactions.

The following prospects exhibit these "different" reactions.

Prospect #2
The Mouse—the Cautious, Quiet Prospect

You know the type: cautious, shy, colorless, won't talk. He's the "salesman's best friend" to some because he's the only one who will let the salesman tell the whole story—without an interruption.

Analyze this type of prospect. Try to determine, is he:

1. Smart? Intelligent? Thoughtful? When he says something, is it important?
2. Dull? Is it that he can't think of anything important to say?

You do this with a question: not a "nice day, isn't it?" question, but one that requires a thoughtful reply. A certain securities salesman uses a question similar to this: "According to our records, Mr. Abbot, you are well-informed on the plastics industry; therefore, what is your reaction to Gerald Frey's recent announcement of the merger of Gow with Polyplastics?" Later: "Do you see increased investment opportunities in this industry?"

Again, let me remind you to *listen* to what the quiet prospect says. Don't worry about what you'll say next. The prospect will give you the clue. Although many salesmen use the question approach with this type of prospect, they become impatient with him and either don't wait for a reply or won't listen to what he says. When you analyze the psychological needs of the "Mouse," you will understand why he gives considerable thought to his answer.

How to Tailor Your Sales Interview

If you find that he is an intelligent person, you can assume that he is purposeful and thrives on order and detail. With this in mind, you will find the best interview is one that appears to be well-organized, one that is very accurate (especially the proof) and uses demonstration whenever possible. He returns to his silent shell if he senses pressure; so go easy on the close. Chances are, he'll close himself. If not, try the minor-point close.

If he is a rather dull prospect, you'll want to keep the interview very simple and short. Work with one benefit that he thinks important. A stronger close may be necessary e.g., two or three minor points. If you must call on him regularly, have a reasonable call objective for each call. You may agree to do a survey, obtain information about your competitors, get additional samples, etc. He can be sold—it just takes longer. He can become a faithful customer once you win his confidence.

The proof step is the most important part of the interview to the quiet prospect. You must use substantial proof and it must be accurate.

NEEDS

Now let's determine what basic needs the Mouse is trying to fulfill—the needs that account for his behavior. First, refer back to the List of Basic Needs on page 72. You probably feel that he is responding to the need to know, to learn and to understand. This need is strong in most people. This is fortunate for us, because this is the reason most people see salesmen. In terms of the Pyramid of Needs, you will probably decide that the Mouse is a safety-seeker.

Thus, buying behaviors, or reactions if you prefer, are a result of people trying to satisfy their needs. Furthermore, a classification of needs and their subsequent behaviors gives you a ready mental reference to determine your strategy.

Prospect #3
The Beaver—the Busy, Impatient Prospect

The Beaver is the one prospect who causes you to perform at your worst; yet he probably has greater buying power than any other type. He is the man of action. He makes rapid decisions. He gets things done. He rarely sits down for a sales interview; when he does, he glances at papers on his desk, signs correspondence, places phone calls and fingers objects on his desk. Unless your sales interview is very good, it won't occupy all of his mental resources and he will simply direct part of his thinking elsewhere. Because he expends more physical and mental energy than most men, he probably is or has the potential to become quite successful. Obviously, he can be a very substantial buyer.

The Beaver acts on impulse, often without careful study. He is not very logical in his thinking or buying. He dominates the sales interview and is continually interrupting. Often, the salesman will have trouble getting attention and creating interest.

How to Tailor Your Sales Interview

Cut out the amenities and small jokes. You have only a very few minutes in which to score. A Verifying question is good in the approach: "I understand you're opening a new store in Whitmore. Am I correct?" Follow with a Developmental Question: "If I can show you how you can get double the return on four square feet of shelf space, would you be interested?"

Above all else, make your product presentation very brief. Use one benefit (such as "double the return"). Use Trial Closes to guide you: "Will your requirements for fast turnover be satisfied with this offer?" Use strong, positive proof—very brief.

You usually don't have to close the Beaver; he's already made up his mind. If he decided not to buy, be sure to determine why: He may have misunderstood or there's another benefit more important.

Unlike the Mouse, he likes things to move fast. There's no such thing as a "thoughtful pause." If one creeps in, you've probably lost him. You'll get objections, and some of them will appear to "have teeth in them." Generally, they are not as severe as they sound and are only requests for more information.

NEEDS

What needs motivate the Beaver and account for his different behavior? From the List of Basic Needs, you probably have selected personal achievement and recognition; and from the Pyramid of Needs, you may have decided that self-actualization and, secondly, esteem are most important.

Knowledge of a reaction-type illustrating extreme characteristics (such as the Beaver) will help you understand other prospects who exhibit milder reactions in this area.

Prospect #4
The Sheep—the Undecided Prospect

The Sheep is a follower—not a leader. He is not an innovator and will not decide on a course of action or accept any opinion that is contrary to that of his circle of associates at work or his social group. He feels as uncomfortable with a new idea as he does with a new model automobile. He waits until others try an idea or buy a product and only then does he decide that it's prudent, safe and acceptable for him.

He will listen courteously to your presentation and interact well with you on questions; but if the idea or product is new, he'll clam up at the close. He does buy standard items very willingly if you avoid the "new wrinkles." If you want to develop him as a customer, you may find it best to stay with established items for a while before going into the newer items in your catalog. He can be sold on a one–call, new–item basis, but only if he sees that his buying action is consistent with his inner needs.

How to Tailor Your Sales Interview

Try to keep the survey and presentation as simple as possible. Complexity confuses him. Permissive and Verifying questions are good in the approach. Avoid the "I have an idea . . ." approach. Probe for one need in the areas of reliability, dependability, long life, ease of operation, etc., and stay with it. Determine if your direction is correct with a Trial Close: "Let's see if I understand your position. You have told me the porcelain enamel finish is an advantage to your customers. Is that right?" Stay with this point through the product presentation and follow with a strong proof. "You mentioned porcelain finish earlier. You will be interested with the experience of Jipson Stores with our porcelain finish stoves. In two months last year . . ." Make your proof good. Your sales depend on it. Show him that others have found your product valuable for the reasons he has mentioned.

You must have a carefully thought-out call objective. This type of prospect moves very slowly. You may have to make the sale over several trips. Without a series of call objectives, each call requiring a stronger commitment to the ultimate sale, you can waste much time with the Sheep. If you feel that you have earned the right to close (by uncovering a strong need or problem that your product fulfills or solves), then there is no reason why a strong close cannot be employed. Actually, it may be required.

NEEDS

Without consulting the two lists of needs, you should be able to decide what needs motivate the Sheep. What are they?

Safety seems paramount. He wants to make the right decision. But what is right for him? There is probably no answer to this except to say that a decision has a better chance of being right if it is the same decision that others have made. Therefore, the Sheep follows, because this path seems to ensure a good decision.

There is another need that the follower holds important that is frequently overlooked. This is the need for acceptance, for affiliation, for affection. He won't make decisions that may prove to be unpopular or controversial—that make him different from his work or social group. His buying decisions are calculated to enhance his image, to make him acceptable, to secure or maintain membership in his group, to win affection. This side of the Sheep offers new vistas to the enterprising salesman—some that you will want to explore.

Prospect #5
The Lion—the Domineering Prospect

The Lion is a decided extrovert who takes over the sales interview from the very beginning. He speaks with apparent authority and, right or wrong, believes that he knows more about your product and its application than you do.

He is easy to identify, not only in his manner, but also in his appearance and surroundings. His office is often "lionish": strong colors and massive furniture. There are strong clues to his areas of excellence: animal rug, athletic trophies, community service certificates, etc.

Although it is easy to classify him, be careful of your assessment of him. Some Lions are the genuine article—every bit as important as they act. Others may be pompous windbags—as false as a $19.50 blue–serge suit. It's important to determine the difference. Here's how: The false Lion brings up petty arguments. He is sensitive, easily antagonized. His manner is only a front to cover a rather immature personality.

It is the difference of one man from another that provides you with the means by which you can control the prospect. The false Lion is easily controlled with flattery. Don't try flattery with the real Lion—he won't appreciate it and will probably terminate the interview. Use only genuine compliments with the real Lion, or none at all—they're not necessary.

How to Tailor Your Sales Interview

The "I have an idea for you" approach is good with the Lion. Permissive and Verifying questions are made for him. He is especially vulnerable to Developmental questions. Listen carefully—he'll tell you how he can be sold. You'll find that Evaluative questions will save a lot of time with the Lion as they sum up and direct the interview toward the close.

Don't try to tell him anything. Imply that he already knows, something like this: "As you know, Mr. Smith, the DeLuxe model is equipped with . . ." Ask him for his opinion; it helps him maintain his self-image.

All–important with the Lion is the Survey. Being the dominant person he is, he has recognized problem areas in his present *modus operandi.* Probe for the problem or simply ask him. Build your product presentation on this point, if possible.

Proof is not important to the Lion. He needs no reassurance. If you have found his problem and convinced him that your product is the solution, you won't need to close.

The Lion is fun to sell; but remember, he likes to run with the bit in his teeth and you must control the interview, at least until you find the problem and suggest the solution. This you can do with questions that are especially useful with the Lion.

NEEDS

It's probably apparent to you that the false Lion is motivated by an almost overwhelming need for esteem. Think of the various ways you can give him esteem, not only during the interview, but also as a consequence of buying your product. This is what he wants—give it to him!

It's also obvious that the real Lion is motivated by self-actualization. Show him how your product will overcome one of his problems: lower maintenance, less scrap, increased profit margin, etc. He realizes that he and you have a mutual goal and that he is dependent on salesmen like you to help him solve his problems. The Lion is the best illustration of the general rule that a product presentation alone doesn't sell. But find the problem, the goal toward which both of you are striving, and he'll buy.

Prospect #6
Glad-Hand Charlie—Mr. Wonderful!

Every sales territory has two or three "Charlies." Most salesmen really look forward to calling on them, but this is really a false sense of progress. Charlie really rolls out the welcome mat. He makes you think you are the greatest salesman who ever carried a briefcase, but he's tough to sell.

This type of prospect is easy to meet. He wants to be liked. He's a back-slapping, joke-telling extrovert. His happy frame of mind and friendliness toward you makes you believe that you're his favorite salesman and that he saves all his business for you. Yet, when you check the records, you find that he is one of your poorest customers. You see, Charlie's a good salesman himself. He spends *your* time in jokes and small talk. *He* makes the sale. Before you know it, he's charmed you right out of the office!

How to Tailor Your Sales Interview

There are two tactical problems presented by this prospect: to get him started into the sales dialogue early and to keep him on track. The Demonstration was born for all the Charlies in the world.

First, don't permit him to get all his jokes out of the way before starting. A "Hello, how are you" is enough. Then say, "I have something to show you." Demonstration! If you have no demo, can you develop one—just for Charlie? A Permissive Question is no good, but a Verifying Question is good to give direction. Developmental Questions are good if they're lean and sharp (not lengthy and involved).

If Charlie gets into a story-telling jag, say "Sorry Charlie, but will you hold this for a minute?" If it's a demonstration, get Charlie into the act. If you have no demonstration, get him to figure a cost estimate or simply hold your rate book!

Charlie likes to talk, and you can keep him on track with questions that allow him to talk, *but in the direction that you dictate.* If he should digress from the sale, bring him back on track with a demo or by interrupting "There's something else I want your opinion on . . ." The minor-point close is good with Charlie; but be prepared with several, for he'll try to slip out with a plethora of talk.

You can make the sale with the talkative prospect if you remember his very pronounced psychological needs. Continually make it evident that these needs can be fulfilled with your product or service. This is his vulnerable spot. He goes to great lengths to satisfy these needs.

NEEDS

You should have no trouble in identifying Charlie's needs as affiliation, affection and esteem. He is a good example of an individual's entire personality being shaped by basic psychological needs and desires. If needs are this potent, think how important they can be in forming buying decisions.

Prospect #7
Sweet Old Bob

Think of the meanest, toughest, most disagreeable prospect you call on. That is *S*weet *O*ld *B*ob. (The initials tell you who he is.) If it is a one-time, one-call sales deal, you simply don't go back. "Why bother—there's plenty of good guys around." If he is part of a sales territory, you skip him—"They really don't pay me enough to take that punishment." And this is the way you've handled Sweet Old Bob in the past.

In the future, you're going to call on him. Why not? He buys as does any prospect. And you're going to sell him. Again, why not? With your new-found knowledge, which compels you to go beyond the superficial and probe for inner needs and problems, you can read his mind, you know how he can be sold. Finally, you're going to sell him as much or more than you do Jack Armstrong. And a final why not? Most salesmen won't call on him. You have the field to yourself—practically virgin territory!

Sweet Old Bob likes a good fight and he fights to win from the vantage point of a prospect who can inflate the truth and conduct himself in an insulting manner. The high point of his day is when he can lock horns with a salesman, and his favorite game is the neophyte "peddler" (as he calls us).

SOB will insult you, falsely criticize your product, make disparaging remarks about your company, use foul language, tear up your pamphlets, etc. I can remember the wise counsel I received from a senior salesman, "Doc" Taylor, in my beginning months as a salesman. I had just returned from an encounter with SOB and reported "I'm sick of being insulted by that @%*!" Doc lit his cigar and leaned back and said, "Well sir, I've been in selling for over 30 years. I've had prospects call me a cheat and a liar—even once had one throw me down a flight of stairs. But I don't believe I've ever been insulted!"

If they're not insults, what are they? SOB is merely testing the salesman. I'll admit that he enjoys it; but I have found if I think of his unwelcome comments as "Temper Tests" I am able to roll with the punches. I've found out something else: that he is impressed with the guy who can take it. After his initial explosion, he'll calm down and be easy to handle. I'll allow him a few verbal liberties with my character, product or company if I can get a fat contract that will bind him to me as a business associate to his benefit and mine.

You'll have to give Bob a better sales interview than you would Jack Armstrong. He can be sold only on the basis of *his* interests, *his* desires, *his* needs. The Dynamic Laws are well-designed for Bob; for he is dying to tell someone his opinions of an idea, a problem or a product—even in a belligerent manner. You must get him to talk in the direction of the sale. You must listen to him in order to pick up the thread for your next question. Also, you must do a little "play acting"—appear to like him. Compliment him on his shrewd observations.

How to Tailor Your Sales Interview

The Permissive Question is good, as is the Verifying Question. The latter establishes the direction of the sale. Developmental Questions will stimulate considerable open discussion. Remember, almost any statement you make becomes controversial; so select only those product benefits that are important to him. Trial Close him after each benefit statement by reminding him of his problem: "You mentioned the high noise level of ABC cutters. Our new XYZ is the answer, don't you agree?" In the Proof, flatter his ego: "Your opinion of the quick-drying qualities of Zemo is supported by a recent study at Blank Research. Let me point out . . ." The Minor-Point Close is especially good for Bob. You will need several alternatives (and several closes).

NEEDS

You'll never guess what basic need accounts for Sweet Old Bob's offensive behavior; so I'll tell you. Bob suffers from a particular form of frustration—aggressive frustration. A person becomes frustrated when he experiences barriers between himself and his goal. The goal is often one of acceptance by others in a social or work group, of affiliation as a member with the group. This is Bob's need, but one would never guess this by his behavior.

What a fertile field is the area of need fulfillment for the salesman! By studying his prospect, his reactions and their underlying needs, the salesman cannot only sell easier, but he can also form close business relationships, which pay dividends for years to come.

Learn to Adjust to the Ebb and Flow of Personal Reactions

You may have recognized an exact parallel in one or more of these prospect types with several of your prospects. However, it is not likely. Few people are full-blown Lions or shy Sheep all the time. Personal characteristics and the state of readiness or mental set change in response to our experience of a day or an hour. It is for this reason that you should think of the Mouse, the Beaver, etc., as reactions.

From time to time, you'll find the All-American prospect, Jack Armstrong, may exhibit some of the belligerent reactions of Sweet Old Bob. When Jack loses his halo, stops thinking logically and responds to some recent event that frustrates his normal need for acceptance and affiliation, you'll know how to handle him. For this call at least, you'll remain calm and will not come unglued with a personal rebuff. You'll listen to him carefully and compliment him on his observation. This simple act of yours will allow him to get it off his chest and the two of you can settle down to business. Your understanding and patience will strengthen the bond of business friendship that you enjoy with Jack.

Some day, even cautious Mr. Mouse may experience some reassurance of his basic need for safety and security and react like the Lion. When you observe this reaction, you will quickly adjust your sales strategy and bolster his ego by asking his opinion.

The Beaver, because he acts on impulse, may have been "stung" on the last order he placed with a salesman. When you call on him, he may be reacting to this experience by being very careful and cautious. He is reacting to the need for safety and you will respond with the reassurance that he is making the right move.

When you call on Glad-Hand Charlie next, he may have his belongingness and affection wants fairly well-gratified. He may react by trying to maintain a favorable self-image. In other words, he'll react normally, as you or I would. You will then use your standard sales strategy.

What an interesting study—the study of people and their needs—and a highly profitable one too, but only if you work at it every day. Let it be your "Learning Tree." Gordon Parks, in his fictionalized autobiography of a Negro boy, quoted his wise mother:

> Some people are good and some of them are bad—just like the fruit on a tree—think of it like that till the day you die—let it be your Learning Tree.*

---

*Gordon Parks, *The Learning Tree* (Harper & Row: New York, N.Y., 1963).

12

How to Get Into Today's Ten Biggest Opportunities with the Dynamic Laws of Salesmanship

Here are the ten biggest opportunities in selling today. Each will give you new sales power; each will set you apart from ordinary salesmen. Properly used, they can be converted into increased sales and commissions. They point the way; but as always, it's up to you to make them work.

Isn't it strange that most of us think of opportunities in the *past* tense? "I could have bought any amount of this sand and cactus country at $20 an acre 15 years ago," said a friend of mine as we drove through a suburb of Phoenix. "Guess what, Mary," called a salesman to his wife as he read the company mail, "Chuck Jones is our new sales manager. We started out together ten years ago—in the same training class." This isn't opportunity. It may be hindsight; it may be reproach; but it isn't opportunity.

Opportunity is only here and now—*present* tense. Chances are, at this very minute you don't see yourself surrounded with opportunities; but you are. If past history has any value at all, it serves to remind you of this fact. Your history, in retrospect, was full of possibilities for investment, education, goal achievement, etc., whether or not you recognized them. We are so busy putting out the daily brush fires that we can't or don't take a long-range view of our position—where we want to go in life and what we're willing to sacrifice to get there.

Each of the ten opportunities presented in this chapter may not be tailor made for you; but don't be too quick to discard any of them. As you read each opportunity, try to apply it to your situation. Is there some element of it you can use? Can you modify? Rearrange? Make smaller? Make larger? Combine?

Finally, when you have completed the chapter, review each opportunity and set some priorities. Which one will make the greatest contribution toward your goal? Which one just seems to fit? Go about this systematically and with purpose. If you do this, I promise you that you can substantially increase your sales success, no matter how successful you have been in the past. And that's only the beginning. Where do you want to go? It's all in your hands; and here are your opportunities.

#1: The Principle of Allocation of Effort

Only a few significant efforts are responsible for the achievements of the majority of results.

What It Means: The Law has wide application. It was originally postulated by Vilfredo Pareto (1848–1923), who was an engineer. Peter Drucker has more recently advanced it as a controlling principle of effective management. Applied to selling, it says that of the total of everything you do and say as a salesman, only a relatively small proportion of your effort (about 20%) achieves about 80% of the results.

Hard to believe? Yes indeed. As a matter of fact, at this time, you are probably bristling with indignation. Eighty percent of your effort is being wasted! Let me call a few facts to your attention: In most major sales forces, 20% of the total salesmen sell 80% of the firm's goods. Probably 20% of your customers are responsible for 80% of your total volume (if you're well established). If you have a number of items in your catalog, 20% of them carry 80% of the firm's total volume. If you close only two out of ten prospects, your close ratio supports the 20/80 principle. You can probably find exceptions to this principle because there may not be sufficient items in your sample. An exception does not nullify the rule; instead, it proves it.

I have found this principle applicable in my daily life as a salesman, sales manager, teacher, consultant, father and husband. It continually challenges me to identify those efforts that really produce results—so that I can repeat or enlarge upon them. By "efforts" I mean many sales efforts: a particular prospecting method; an effective approach or close; a particular kind of customer; pre-planning; etc.

What about the 80% of effort that achieves only 20% of the results? This is what costs you money in missed sales and wasted time. It is generally sheer busyness. Our ego is strangely involved in this area. We do certain things because we've always done them this way (supports our need for security), or because we evolved a procedure (esteem) or because "all the other guys do it" (belongingness).

The lesson to be learned is to substitute productive activities for the "busyness" activities. This calls for deep soul searching and complete honesty. Not many salesmen are capable of being this truthful with themselves. I hope you are.

For Example: Cliff Hanger (not his real name) had been bucking for promotion into the home office for over a year. A salesman with a great deal of creative imagination, he tried to call attention to himself by submitting many sales promotion ideas to the sales manager. Some of his ideas were quite good and his company certainly needed a man with his imagination in the home office. However, there was divided opinion as to his qualifications because his sales volume was deplorable. Finally, Cliff became frustrated and decided to resign and get another job where his "ability would be appreciated."

This is where I came into the picture. I encouraged Cliff to honestly appraise his situation. He concluded that many of his brainstorms were fulfilling egoistic goals and were draining off much of his time and energy (part of the 80% busyness segment), but were not contributing toward goal achievement. As he had already established his reputation as an "idea man," his continuing investments in this area were not producing results. Instead, he substituted efforts designed to increase his sales volume (the 20% area). He was a better–than–average salesman and he saw an outlet for his creativeness in helping his customers (retail merchants) solve their problems through better displays, merchandising and clerk training. Within a year, Cliff's sales volume doubled and he received his coveted advancement to sales promotion manager in the home office.

HOW CAN YOU USE THIS PRINCIPLE?

With a pencil and paper, do an honest appraisal of yourself in terms of your expenditures of time and effort toward result achievement. Where do you want to go? What results are necessary to get there? Identify some of the things you like to do (and may do very well) but aren't really contributing toward results. Ask yourself "What would happen if I didn't do so-and-so?" If the answer is "Nothing," consider scrapping it. In short, try to eliminate as many non-productive activities as possible and try to enlarge as many productive activities as possible.

#2: The Principle of Conservation of Time

Tomorrow never comes. Results are achieved by crowding as much purposeful activity into today as possible.

What It Means: If you knew that when the sun goes down today your life, as you know it, would come to a close, you would probably begin to examine your value systems and redirect your efforts to be a better husband, a better father, or a better salesman. Do you, in fact, have any assurance that this may not be true? But you argue that your experience has shown that every day follows the one that preceded it. You have faith the cycle will continue for many years.

So there we have it: We spend time—life's most precious commodity—as if we had plenty of it, when in truth it's in very short supply. Most people live today as if they were going to get a second chance at it.

Look at it this way: If you have a goal of earning $20,000 or $40,000 or any other figure, would you be satisfied if this goal were achieved in 24 months? Of course not. The specification of 24 months has the effect of reducing the goal by 50%. An income goal always has a time dimension to make it significant. Very successful men impose a time dimension on the more mundane operational aspects of their work life as a form of self discipline—to force them to use the most effective techniques to get work done. Because they respect time, they achieve success.

In the Hawaiian Islands, there is the legend of Maui, a demigod who was troubled by the swift passage of the sun across the skies, not allowing the crops to mature. He went to the great mountain and, as the sun's rays crept over it, he snared them with seven ropes. "Give me my life," pleaded the sun. "I will give you your life if you promise to go more slowly across the sky," said Maui. To this day, the sun is careful to go slowly across the heavens; and the great mountain is known as *Haleakala*—the House of the Sun.

For Example: The seven "ropes" you can use to lengthen the day might be these:

1. Have a Goal: You should have a goal for each increment of time, from a five-year goal, down through annual goals, to quarterly, monthly, weekly and daily goals. Put some "reach" in each—above your present performance.

2. Pre–plan: Decide on what you need to reach these goals: more education, increased skills, greater market penetration, more customers, more prospects. Prepare for each call through observation. Decide what additional knowledge you need from your prospects. Set call objectives.

3. Expand your Day: Chances are good that you can make one or two more calls a day. (This alone could mean a 25% increase in income.) Where can you get the time: at the beginning, the middle or the end?

4. Exclude Interruptions: Exclude personal errands (laundry, car repairs, etc.), two-hour lunches with fellow salesmen, long coffee breaks, favors to customers (do them on Saturday), long waiting for customers.

5. Examine Your Routing: Some salesmen spend over 50% of their time driving. Drive at night and early in the morning. Make appointments in one section of the city. The name of the game is "selling," not "driving."

6. Cut Out the Hogwash: You'll get into more offices if you establish a reputation for being a businessman. Make your sales interviews short, to the point. Practice Second-Person Sensitivity. Talking 15 minutes about football and five minutes about business is stupid!

7. Find More Time For Relaxation: Spend more time for your favorite sport. Spend more time with your wife and kids. Spend more time for self improvement. This is one of the benefits of better time management.

HOW CAN YOU USE THIS PRINCIPLE?

Jot down the "time wasters" in your operation. Are there things you enjoy doing and even consider highly desirable that occupy considerable time during your sales day but do not contribute to goal achievement? Many of them you deem important only because they are ego–satisfying. Where can you find another two hours a day that you can use more effectively? *Learn to invest in your personal goals.*

#3: The Principle of Resistance to Change

When people are unwilling to change, insist that they at least be willing to test an idea.

What It Means: The instances of resistance to change in selling are legendary. They are your constant companion throughout your sales day; so much so, that salesmen are often referred to as "change artists." You work to bring about change: change from a competitor's services, change from an older procedure, change from small orders to larger orders, etc. The reason the changes you seek are so hard to bring about are that they involve egoistic needs—a need for security, for acceptance, for approval. People keep these needs pretty well covered; but at the same time, they like to think of themselves as reasonably broad-minded. This is where "testing an idea" has special appeal to a prospect. It allows him to maintain his former position of security and yet it caters to his need to know, to understand. Once you get a prospect to test an idea, he feels that the risk of change has been largely removed. He thinks *he* discovered the idea.

For Example: Some of the ideas I have presented to you in this book have been difficult for you to accept. I know that if they had been presented to me during several stages of my development as a salesman, I would say, as I'm sure you have, "That might work for some salesmen—but not for me. My type of selling is different, my territory is different, my product is different," etc. However, I'd have the uneasy feeling that I might be overlooking a good thing and that, if I expected to overcome resistance to change in my customers, I'd better start with myself.

Testing an idea is the answer. This is what I want you to do—test some of these ideas. I think I have as much right to ask this of you as you have to ask it of a customer.

When we test a new product in a market, we try to make all the conditions under which it will be tested as identical to actual marketing conditions as possible. I ask you (as you should ask your customers) not to unduly influence the favorable or unfavorable outcome of the test. Don't prejudge the test.

HOW TO USE THIS PRINCIPLE

1. Select five ideas in this book that seem to promise advantages to you. Set priorities. Use one idea a week and test it. You may want to make some adjustments or modifications.

2. What are the areas of prospect resistance that bother you? How can you incorporate the strategy of "testing an idea" into your sales interview?

#4: The Principle of Unified Action

A salesman can't sell until he has the same goals as the prospect.

What it Means: Frequently, a sales conversation is not a meeting of the minds; instead, it is a contest or, at best, a communication of information. Unless the needs, problems or goals of the prospect are fairly accurately known by the salesman, and unless he appeals to them, the prospect will sense that the direction of the sale is moving against him and he will become defensive. This is a natural consequence of the nature of the confrontation: "To buy" means sacrificing a position of strength or security (possession of money) in order to gain a product or service that has (in the prospect's mind) no "value." The salesman creates value when he is able to show that the product satisfies a need or solves a problem or helps the prospect achieve a goal.

Touchdowns are scored only by the team with the ball—only

when they are on offense. Try to keep the prospect from becoming defensive.

There are three critical stages in a sales interview—times when the prospect is more likely to become defensive:

First, during the first few minutes—is the Approach. If you give him the impression that you want to sell him a product (not satisfy a need or solve a problem), he'll become defensive. The second critical stage is when you recite product benefits (many of which mean nothing to him if you don't know his needs). The third important point is just prior to the close, when he isn't "sold" and he senses he'll soon be required to make a decision.

Defensiveness takes two forms: covert and overt. In the covert (hidden) form, the prospect says nothing (maybe he wasn't given the opportunity to talk!) but simply doesn't buy. In the overt form, he speaks out, and what he says is called an objection.

Three important points:

1. Make an honest effort to tentatively identify needs in preplanning.
2. Use questions to verify and solicit new information.
3. When objections are voiced, be empathetic—concede that the prospect has a good point.

For Example: Harry D. Cummings (not his real name) sells securities for Diversified Investors, Inc., in Kanopolis, Indiana. He reads the Daily Record for real estate transfers, new corporations formed, etc. He is active in many civic affairs. This is sometimes called "prospecting," but an even bigger dividend to Harry is that he gets to know people—their needs and goals. Here are some questions he uses to verify needs and develop recognition of "value":

"If I could show you how, in ten years, you could have enough money to start a business of your own, would you be interested?"

"I have a study—a comparison between 1,000 private investors and 1,000 mutual-fund investors—which has important investment guidelines for a man in your position. May I show you?"

"From what you've told me, you believe that the funds you have to invest are not large enough to interest a professional investment counselor. Is that correct?"

Occasionally, when the prospect goes on the defensive, Harry gives the ball back to him with such a phrase as, "I certainly can appreciate your position . . ." or "That's an interesting observation. Let's see if I understand. You feel that if . . ."

HOW TO USE THIS PRINCIPLE

What are the needs that your product fulfills? What Development Questions can you ask that will elicit the information you need from the prospect? What aspects of his appearance, office and past buying action afford valuable clues as to his needs? How can I interpret what he tells me into needs, wants, and problems?

#5: The Principle of Value Recognition

The act of "value recognition" is strictly an afferent phenomenon: A person has to recognize it himself; he can't be told.

What it Means: When the salesman accurately identifies a need and verifies it, he gets the prospect to think about the need. He next suggests satisfaction of that need with a developmental question. He then bridges from *need* to showing how it can be fulfilled with his product and, in so doing, he creates a vacuum that the prospect promptly fills by recognizing value. This is a well-known psychological principle (principle of closure) in which the subject tries to complete the picture. Value recognition for the prospect is strictly a "do-it-yourself" project.

The difference between the clothing salesman's glib remark: "This suit will make you the most distinguished man in the office" and the prospect's recognition of the same hopeful promise is one of acceptance. The salesman's comment is rejected; whereas, the prospect readily agrees to his own summation because it was his own conclusion. This is "value recognition."

This same psychological technique is employed in education. The Discovery Technique says that when a student "discovers" or arrives at a conclusion, he accepts it and remembers it. He wasn't told.

For Example: When William C. Durant was building the General Motors Corporation, he wanted to persuade a particularly capable but "bull-headed" engineer to use a new idea on the assembly line. He knew he could give the engineer a direct order but he also knew the engineer would try to see that the idea failed. Knowing the engineer had a great need to feel important, he told him of an opportunity he had to write an article for a trade journal on the new assembly line system. He went on to describe the system and, as he did, he hinted that he'd like to have the engineer author the article. Before Durant could finish, he was interrupted by the engineer who eagerly cried out, "Say, that's something we can use on our line."

HOW TO USE THIS PRINCIPLE

As a start, try to construct a sales interview moving from identification of need . . . to verification . . . to a Developmental Question. Notice how natural it is for the prospect to "complete the picture." Test the idea with another salesman or with your wife.

#6: The Principle of Untapped Potential

The salesman himself creates his own productive or unproductive sales environment.

What It Means: A salesman, by changing his basic assumptions, can actually change the nature of the "world" he experiences. He exerts a powerful influence over the prospect by virtue of the "We Affinity" phenomenon. "We Affinity" is the result of his perceptions—the observation, investigation and interrogation—which disclose needs and goals and the problems that lie between. It results in an emphatic interaction between salesman and prospect.

Numerous sensitivity studies have been conducted at the Harvard Research Center and elsewhere that have shown that a person has it within his power to determine how he will be received by another person. This technique has been reliable in between 70% and 85% of the subjects studied!

This concept has exciting possibilities when it is considered in relation to Dr. William James' assertion that most people are using only 10% of their full capacities. It is entirely possible that we can tap unexpected potential within ourselves and others.

To the practicing salesman, accustomed to the realities of a tough sales situation, this may be hard to swallow. But remember, whether you realize it or not, you already make certain basic assumptions about your prospect and you deal with him on the basis of what you conceive him to be. What I ask in the future is that you change those basic assumptions—correct them in line with the facts you learn by careful observation and investigation or even keep them "open" until more facts are obtained through interrogation. If you will do this, you will develop an interractive "homing" device, which will direct your words and gestures toward creating value for your product in the mind of your customer. When he clearly sees "value" (satisfaction of a need with your product), he buys!

For Example: A friend of mine, an electronics expert whom I'll call Jim Lane, had designed, built and patented a new type of antenna. It was the antenna, manufactured in his shop, that brought him a living. Jim had been approached several times to sell, but somehow the deal would always fall through.

The other party to this true account I will call Swanson—the president of a large electronics firm. Swanson wanted to buy Jim's company, and made an investigation before approaching him. He found that Jim detested business details (hiring, payroll, bookkeeping, etc.), that he distrusted big business because he thought it stifled creative work and that, despite his personal attraction to independent work, he was worried about the insecurity this life imposed on his family.

During the negotiations, Swanson pointed out the greater opportunities Jim would have if he could be relieved of the details of running a business and could devote his full time to development. Furthermore, with the sale of the business, Jim would receive stock in Swanson's firm, thus ensuring long-range security.

The result was that both parties to the negotiation benefited. Swanson gained a valuable specialty product and a company to manufacture it. Also, he gave valuable time to an expert who had not yet reached his full creative potential. Lane had his major needs satisfied: He need not spend time on the petty details of business, he would be able to continue his creative work and he acquired greater financial security.

Each man benefited in his particular way. The "We Affinity" was the guideline as each strived toward a mutual goal. In so doing, each man afforded the other an opportunity to reach a fuller potential.

Other companies had tried to buy Jim's company; but Swanson succeeded because of knowledge of human nature, preparation, strategy—all combined to satisfy needs and create value.

HOW TO USE THIS PRINCIPLE

What percentage of your potential are you using at the present time? 10%–20%–30%? Can you see how the "We Affinity" can permit you to use more of your potential? Test the idea. Select a customer you know pretty well. Think through a sales dialogue with him. If you feel confident in your mind, try it the next time you call.

#7: The Principle of Dissonance

A person strives to resolve dissonance and is inclined to accept a reasonable escape when it is offered. Dissonance is inharmony, discord, disagreement, indecision.

What It Means: Dissonance is disturbing to people. The prospect suffers from dissonance when he thinks: "It sounds good. But can I believe the salesman? There must be something I don't see in this proposition, or I'd have thought of it before. Is there some aspect of this proposition that can trip me up?" This is the dissonance of belief.

The dissonance of decision occurs later in the interview. It's the "I'd sure like to buy that red sports job . . . But maybe I should be practical and buy the family sedan . . . Or save my money . . . After all, with Mary starting college this fall . . . But the tires on the old jalopy are getting smooth . . ." and so it goes. The prospect feels uncomfortable.

When the prospect resolves dissonance, he feels relieved. The salesman can be of welcome help to the prospect at these times; and this spells opportunity.

The salesman has a wonderful opportunity when he senses dissonance in his prospect, for the prospect eagerly accepts any reasonable way out. To dispel the dissonance of belief, the salesman in effect says "Here is an impartial third party who is today enjoying the benefits I have just described." Salesmen, by their very nature, are suspect; but an unknown third party somehow has credibility.

In the dissonance of decision, the prospect is on the "horns of a dilemma." He doesn't want to say "Yes" and (believe it or not) most prospects strongly resist saying "No." To remove himself from this uncomfortable position, he says to the salesman, "I want to think it over" or "I want to talk with our people." If the salesman misses here, he misses a real opportunity. True, consultation is sometimes necessary; if so, agree to some pretext (getting more information, for example) to schedule another call. If it is a stall, *reinstate the dissonance.* Review benefits and close on a Minor Point. He may agree to a color selection, when he won't agree to a "Yes."

For Example:

The Dissonance of Belief: "Here is a report from the Agricultural College of the state university that illustrates the increased yield you can expect from this hybrid. Next year, you can have these yields."

"Phil Jennings at Central Gun had a problem similar to the one you described. He purchased the XL unit seven months ago. Here is a report of his operating costs during the last quarter. It illustrates the savings . . . Is that what you had in mind?"

The Dissonance of Decision: "Mr. Jones, you have just told me that you want to think it over. Fine! Let's think it through together and when we've finished I'm going to ask for a *definite decision.* If you say "No," that's perfectly OK. If you say "Yes," here are the benefits you'll start enjoying . . . Mr. Jones, just one more question: Which model, the 100-gallon capacity or the 75-gallon is best suited to your needs?"

HOW TO USE THIS PRINCIPLE

Think back on a typical sales encounter. How often do you let your prospects "slip off the hook" by not making any definite decision? Once you recognize dissonance, show the prospect an attractive alternative, which puts you further ahead in the sale. Practice these two techniques in several dry runs before using them.

#8: The Principle of Empathy

To move another person to action, you must project yourself into his state of mind and learn what arguments will stir the response you want.

What It Means: Empathy is a bridge to understanding. No salesman should be without this insight; for it says to the prospect in loud, unspoken language, "I'm more interested in you—your needs, your problems—than I am in me or my product." The prospect and his needs take center-stage-front and the salesman and product become supporting actors. The "We Affinity" is a state of mind the prospect senses through the salesman's approach and subsequent steps in the sales process. When the salesman sees the critical issues through the prospect's eyes, he can make appeals that make good sense to the prospect. This is more than *rapport,* (a harmonious or sympathetic relationship and largely dependent on personality); it is *empathy,* a deeper feeling. Again, sympathy is a "feeling *for";* empathy is a "feeling *with.*" No longer does a sales contact take on the complexion of a contest; now it becomes a mutual undertaking.

For Example: John Delany (not his real name) felt stymied after his first call on George Crosier, Vice President of the Condyle Company. Here was a man within 18 months of retirement who apparently just wanted to ride out the remaining months without any problems. Yet he controlled the decision of accepting or rejecting the proposal of the First Midland Bank and Trust to computorize the billing, inventory and payroll functions at Condyle. Look at the problem through Crosier's eyes? John came up with a blank: "If I were in Crosier's shoes, maybe I wouldn't want to make waves either with only 18 months to go."

Just by chance, several weeks later, he found himself talking with the Public Relations Director of Condyle at a cocktail party. The P-R man brought up the subject, "Why don't you visit with us John? We certainly need someone to take a hard look at our billing and accounting procedures." John told him that Crosier hadn't exactly rejected the idea but was blocking the acceptance of his proposal. The P-R man told him that Crosier, the son of the founder, had spent all his work life in frustration because he knew he'd never be elected President, even though he was a capable man of ambition. This and other bits of information, plus John's review of his first meeting with Crosier, gave him the insight he wanted. He began to think of the computer system as a vehicle for the attainment of Crosier's goals.

In a conference two weeks later, John obtained approval for the first phase—a preliminary study. What was the magic? It was the "We Affinity," which directed Crosier's thinking toward accomplishing a computer installation at Condyle in 18 months and, in so doing, leaving a memorial to his ability and foresight. The "We Affinity"—a bridge to understanding—a working together toward a common goal.

HOW TO USE THIS PRINCIPLE

Try to put yourself in the shoes of your prospect. Try to look at yourself and your product as the prospect would. What more information do you need? Every sales problem has a solution; and empathy will help you find it.

#9: The Principle of Rational Requirements

Rational requirements must be present to make the sale, but they do not in themselves make the sale.

What It Means: By rational requirements we mean price, quality, delivery, availability, credit terms, etc.—the necessary requirements for a sale to be made. At one time in America's sales history, they were important differentials; and the success or failure of a sales contact depended largely upon them. However, as competition increased in almost all fields, they became less important determinents in making the sale. How many Kenmore washers would Sears & Roebuck sell if Montgomery Ward's Signature washers were more desirable in price or quality? The economic facts of life make it necessary for a company to produce and market a product at the "best" price, quality, delivery, availability, credit terms, etc.—just to stay in business. But this doesn't guarantee that it will sell.

You may feel that your product has a definite advantage. It may be either price or quality or both. If these requirements *are* advantages, you are more than ever dependent upon your ability to develop the "We Affinity." If your price is lower, don't become too dependent on this advantage to sell the product for you. Customers who buy on price alone are "temporary" customers who can be lured away by any weekend special.

For Example: The following is a letter from Rick Johns (not his real name), a relatively new salesman for a farm implement company, to his sales manager. It is symptomatic of a salesman's over-reliance on rational requirements.

> I know my sales have not been anything to write home about, but I have been making the calls. If I may be frank, most of our stuff is priced too high. I lose a lot of business to Springer, who has us beat by at least 10%, which is a lot of money to most farmers today. When I told you about Jim Urbank who wanted to buy six windrowers, you did give me a competitive price and Jim ordered one and promised to order more but he never has. If you could give me a more competitive price, I'm sure I could sell a lot more customers.

HOW TO USE THIS PRINCIPLE

We as salesmen hear objections based on rational requirements all day long—so much so that we begin to believe them ourselves. When voiced by a prospect, they are usually a symptom of your not having uncovered the hidden personal needs, organizational goals or problems to be solved. Practice probing deeper; for this is where the sale is to be found.

#10: The Principle of Differentials

People are interested in the differences in things—not the sameness of things. They buy differences—differences that appeal to them.

What It Means: To a prospect, the real differential is the salesman—his ability to sense the needs and aspirations of the prospect and the ability to translate the features of his product into specific benefits that promise satisfaction of those needs.

This is a rare ability. That's why it is a differential today. It can be learned by starting with a basic knowledge of the needs of people and building through practice in the arts of investigation, observation and interrogation. One can develop a sixth sense—an intuitive feeling that communicates itself to the prospect and allows the salesman to virtually "read the prospect's mind."

This changes the emphasis from the product to the prospect. The approach is not "I want to talk to you about our new Widget"; instead, it is "I have an idea that can result in . . . (reaching a personal or organizational goal)."

Other differentials may exist in the product itself. A higher cost is a differential that has real sales power if it can be translated by the empathetic salesman into need-satisfaction (greater security or more esteem, for example). Some prospects see a differential between two popular makes of cars. Why do they? Both are excellent vehicles with comparable economy, appearance, etc. The answer is found in the discerning salesman as he probes for motivations: "Other guys at the plant have them" (Belongingness needs); "I was just made Vice President" (Esteem needs); "I want to save money" (Security needs).

For Example: At the time General Motors decided to enter the "small, economy car" field, the market was dominated by Henry Ford, who had 90% of the market with his "Tin Lizzie" selling at a figure so low that General Motors couldn't possibly compete at that price level. Henry was depending entirely on his favorable position on price (a rational requirement) to maintain his position even to the point of declaring "We'll produce cars in any color—just so it's black."

General Motors successfully invaded Ford's sanctuary—with a car priced $200 higher! They did so by offering differentials: colors, detachable rims, a self-starter.

HOW TO USE THIS PRINCIPLE

After having studied these Dynamic Laws of Motivation, you should have a pretty good idea of what your differential is. If you can make a commitment to yourself at this time, you have set yourself apart from the many salesmen who never do come to grips with the hard facts of sales life. *You are the differential.* You can achieve your sales goals.

There is one last point I want to make. You have been introduced to the various, dynamic sales techniques that have worked well for me and for the thousands of salesmen I have supervised, trained and counseled. However, merely having read and studied the Dynamic Laws will not bring success. The time has come when you must set these Laws in motion.

In the years ahead, you can make remarkable progress and enjoy selling more than ever before; but despite the direction given you in the Dynamic Laws, I know that sales progress and enjoyment are essentially do-it-yourself projects.

As you strive to bring about changes in buying behavior on the part of your prospects, you must stimulate changes in selling behavior on your part; and this calls for a high degree of self-discipline. You must practice tough-minded salesmanship—an attitude directed toward self improvement.

Most of our present sales techniques are the product of hard times. We have enjoyed abundance and wealth for a few short years: 50 years is at most a very short period of time in the total of human experience. Times have changed. Today, things are changing faster than we can comprehend; but some of our sales habits have not changed. We live in a time when few people buy because of rational requirements. Old sales habits die hard; but change they must. I suggest to you that you can accelerate your change by simply testing a few new ideas. I hope you see the opportunities that lie ahead and that you will be equal to the challenge that is yours.

Index

D

E

F

G

H

I

T